Journey Against One Current

The Spiritual Autobiography of a Chinese Christian

Zhi-Dao "Julia" Duan
with Judith Palpant

William Carey Library

P.O. BOX 40129
PASADENA, CALIFORNIA 91114

Published by
WILLIAM CAREY LIBRARY
P. O. Box 40129
Pasadena, CA 91114
Phone (818) 798-0819

Library of Congress Cataloging-in-Publication Data

Duan, Julia.
    Journey against one current : the spiritual autobiography of a Chinese Christian / Julia Duan.
       p.   cm.
    ISBN 0-87808-273-5
    1. Duan, Julia.   2. Christian biography--China.   I. Title.
    BR1725.D715A3   1997
    275.1'082'092--dc21
    [B]   97-27487
                                               CIP

Cover design and illustrations by Esther Cochran

Printed in the United States of America

Contents

104461

List of Illustrations

Foreword

Julia Duan was one of the first Chinese Christians I met upon my return to Nanjing University in China, after one year's study at Whitworth College in Spokane, Washington. Meeting her was an answer to my prayers. As a newly baptized Christian, I feared returning to my homeland with no opportunity of fellowship with Christians. Dr. and Mrs. Frank Houser from Whitworth College, then teaching at Nanjing University, introduced me to Julia, a Christian professor on campus, and her home soon became the place where I enjoyed fellowship. Despite its inadequate physical conditions, her simple dwelling was inviting and full of warmth to those who thirsted for the knowledge of God. Julia inspired us young Christians with her love for Christ and enthusiasm to spread the Gospel.

As a young Christian from a much different generation, I've found that reading Julia's story has been a rewarding experience. I was fascinated by the missionary work Julia witnessed in her early years. Chinese people of my generation have had little or no knowledge of the missionaries' work in China, due to lack of documentation in Chinese. This book offers us an opportunity to be touched by the missionaries' love for Christ, by their compassion for the Chinese, and by their willingness to suffer with them. Julia's book also gives an account of war and political upheavals in China. Reading her book enables me to learn a part of our nation's history in a more personal way. For a long time, I made a conscious effort to avoid reading any books about this era in contemporary China. I learned from previous experience that writings describing the pain and suffering of that time leave readers with deep emotional burdens. I am grateful to revisit that era with Julia and see it in a new light. I found myself beginning to embrace that part of our history which I once avoided for fear of pain. Through Julia's eyes I see the joy of experiencing God's love more deeply and profoundly in the midst of suffering.

Knowing Julia is a privilege. Her life is a testimony to God's love and faithfulness. He provided when she was in need. He protected her when her life was endangered. He healed her sickness and bound up her wounds. He renewed her strength and put new songs in her mouth. May her stories encourage those who long to experience God's love and tender mercies.

G. Y.
Portland, 1997

Preface

So amazing is God's grace that has saved me and guided me all the way through my life. He has been holding my hand through all my dark and trying days, and set my feet in His blessed ways. When I was 73 years of age, His strong hand miraculously led me to obtain a visa, never before issued under such circumstances, so that I could study religion at Whitworth College in Spokane, Washington.

I was somewhat surprised when Professor Linda Hunt suggested that I write out my life story. I longed to testify to God's working in my life, but I was unsure of my ability. Struggling on the computer, I learned bit by bit with the great help of Kenneth Pecka and Jason Vergara at Whitworth College, as well as Greg Gaertner and Darryl Boyd at Moody Bible Institute. From the spring of 1993 on to early 1995, while I was studying successfully at Whitworth College and at Moody, I managed to write all the chapters of my story in broken English.

I want to thank my good friend Judy Palpant who collaborated in deliberations, pruning and final touches to prepare the manuscript for publication. I also wish to thank Professor Linda Hunt for her continued involvement as well as Dr. Roger Mohrlang for his academic advising and Bible classes. Dr. Terry McGonigal was a source of encouragement and support. The project was brought to completion with the fine help of Dr. James Emery, Michael Hermanson and Northwest Maps, Inc. of Spokane.

I appreciate Diane Hermanson, Ellen Gephart, Dr.

Frank and Mrs. Helen Houser, and many others who have helped me in various ways and made this labor possible. Finally, I want to thank my Heavenly Father God, who chose to use a trifling vessel as unworthy as I.

Thanks to all! Thanks to God! May His will be done. Amen!

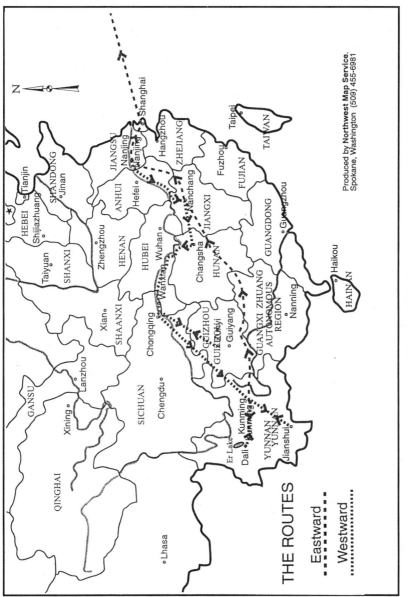

Map of China

Kunming City, Anning County and Surrounding Area

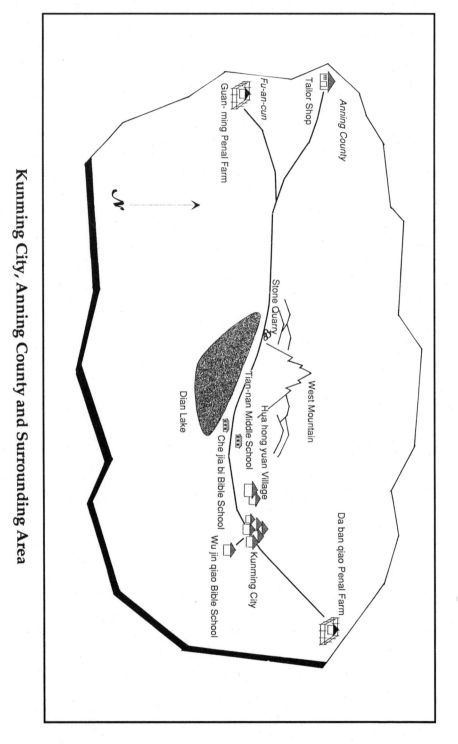

Anning County
Tailor Shop
Fu-an-cun
Guan-ming Penal Farm
N
Stone Quarry
Dian Lake
West Mountain
Tian-nan Middle School
Hua hong yuan Village
Che jia bi Bible School
Wu jin qiao Bible School
Kunming City
Da ban qiao Penal Farm

Part I
In Preparation
預備

Plum

Endures bitter weather,
symbolizes strength, perseverance, and fearlessness.

蒙 恩

1
Saved in a Crisis

To entrust someone with a great task, Heaven is sure first to toil one's bones and muscles, suffer one's will and mind, starve one's body and skin...and then give them the task.
Mencius (Fourth-century Chinese philosopher)

But the dove found no resting place for the sole of her foot, and she returned into the ark to him, for the waters were on the face of the whole earth. So he put out his hand and took her, and drew her into the ark to himself   Gen. 8:9

The war came too soon for me. It cut me off from all my dreams. I stared down into the churning waters of the Yangtze River as the steamer plied the waves, carrying us upstream. Siezed by deep concern, I found it hard to push against the emotional current that pressed down.

It had been just three days since I received a telegram from my sisters-in-law, saying, "Your husband has been in a bus accident en route to Chongqing from Zunyi."

A bus accident? How was he wounded? Why didn't he send me word? There was no answer, of course, only a vast haziness in my mind. The midnight wind grew colder; I went back inside the cabin to my berth, where Mao-Mao, my 16-month-old daughter, slept peacefully.

By late next afternoon, anticipation mounted as we approached our destination, the city of Chongqing. It sat up high where the Yangtze River and the Jialing River meet, and it appeared to be an impenetrable fortress. No wonder the government had moved the country's capital

from the vulnerable coast of Nanjing to this protected inland location. The steamship anchored and the passengers poured onto the riverbank, absorbed by the mass
of houses and small shops hugging the hillside.

After two days on the steamship, it felt good to step
onto solid ground again. My heart was comforted knowing I was now only another two day's journey away from
my husband. MaoMao and I were carried in a sedan
chair to ascend the several hundred, ancient stone steps
to the city. I paid the carriers and headed straight for the
bus station.

By April of 1939 the war had increased the hustle and
bustle of the throngs in the streets. The people pressed in
upon MaoMao and me. We stood in line to get information on the next possible bus to Zunyi. By the time I
reached the window, a frazzled ticket agent informed me
that I could not get a seat for at least three days. He sold
me the ticket and told me my number would be posted
the day of departure. I felt relieved to have the matter settled. Yet I could not deny the keen disappointment
knowing three long days stretched ahead of me.

Chongching's perpetual gray sky matched my dull
spirit. Friends tried valiantly to distract me by taking me
sightseeing. Because the city was terraced, we sometimes
climbed stone steps to get from one level to another. At
other times, we hired rickshaws and traveled the roads
which circled up around the outskirts of the city. I was
unaccustomed to hilly terrain and was astonished to see
the rickshaw runners doggedly pull the two-wheeled
carts slowly uphill. At the top of the hill, they deftly tilted
the poles back and hung onto them like acrobats for the
trip downhill at breakneck speed. I vividly remember
gripping the sides of the rickshaw while MaoMao held
on to me for dear life.

Despite the sightseeing trips, I found myself growing
more and more impatient. On the last day my friends

suggested we visit a fortuneteller. Out of curiosity, I agreed to join them. Of course, the fortuneteller lived in a beautiful home. Riches gleaned from desperate clients allowed him to live among the elite. We were ushered into the drawing room. There the fortuneteller studied my face and the palms of my hands. I, in turn, searched his countenance and awaited his words. He spoke in vague generalities, and I knew his glib prophecies were oft repeated with other clients. I left in frustration.

The following day my journey resumed. The bus roared as it slowly climbed the muddy, rugged hill en route to Zunyi of Guizhou Province. MaoMao slept comfortably in my arms. I gazed at the pelting raindrops beating against the windows, paying no attention to the mountainous terrain outside, nor to the passengers' noisy gossip on the inside. In my thoughts I busily pondered my husband's unfortunate accident. How serious were his injuries? Tenderly kissing my daughter's face, I pulled her close, determined to remain calm until I had found out the truth. With great difficulty the bus crawled up one peak after another. Impatiently, I shut my eyes and remembered this man. How proud I was of him. Better educated than most military officers at age 28, he was already an instructor of tactics in the Zunyi Military College. The last time we talked, he said, "If I survive this war, I will become a successful man." The passengers' murmuring grew to shouts,:

"Death Cliff! Death Cliff!"

"A bus fell over the cliff a few days ago!"

"Six or seven were killed!"

"Military college men."

The bus's roar intensified as it laboriously climbed up a steep, narrow section of road. This must be the place of the accident! My heart sank when I heard some people yelling:

"Many were injured!"

"Relatives came to identify...."

I pulled my shawl around to cover MaoMao, and followed the other passengers as they disembarked and walked to where some new wooden pilings marked the cliff's edge. Peering down into the deep ravine, I spotted a battered old bus sitting motionless, half submerged in water. I overheard someone say the bus had rolled over two or three times as it plummeted to the bottom. Yes, that was his bus. My heart was restless and troubled as I climbed back on the bus and gave my hungry daughter some crackers and a tangerine.

Two agonizing hours later, the bus pulled into Zunyi station. My husband's sisters stepped out from the crowd. I handed MaoMao to their maid, as they each took hold of me by an arm, crying, "Brother is gone! Brother is gone!" My mind was numb, and I could not believe my ears. Then I saw the line of six black coffins half-buried in freshly dug graves. His name was carved on the first one. I realized, "He is IN THERE and I shall NEVER see him again. All his aspirations and ideals have vanished into the void. I am not yet twenty! My poor MaoMao has lost her father...!" A sudden, piercing pain grabbed my heart as darkness engulfed me. I fell to the ground unconscious.

During the next six weeks, I sorted through my husband's possessions. My thoughts moved backward and forward as I grappled with the reality of the situation. The pain deep inside only increased with my daughter's bantering. She could not yet comprehend the loss. I must turn around my adversity and not let her suffer. I was to return to Wanxian.

My husband's sisters were preparing to move on with their children to Tianshui, Gansu Province, to join their husbands, high-ranking military officials. They persisted in trying to persuade me to move with them.

"We will feed and educate MaoMao. She is the only

'blood and bones' of our dear brother!"

As I weighed the options, the tide of my heart went up and down. It seemed the Creator had played a big trick on me, but I would fight my way through life!

In the end, I declined their kind offers of support. I determined to care for MaoMao myself and turn my misfortune around in pursuit of an education. We parted ways. The war carried them to the far northwest region of China as MaoMao and I returned to my middle school, where I passed the final exam just in time to graduate. How good it was to see my friends and teachers again. Later that summer we returned to Chongching, where I took the national college entrance exam. With all the turmoil in my life, it was no surprise when I failed. I had always been outstanding in my class and was accustomed to winning contests in speech, music, drama and sports! With the door shut on further education I had no alternative but to do odd jobs just to survive.

I took in a simple village girl to care for MaoMao while I worked. We lived in a rented room. Our circumstances, one after another, were not favorable. The Japanese army had first attacked Shanghai on August 13, 1937. The violent war spread rapidly. Now, the Japanese occupied most of eastern China, where my family lived, so I was cut off from them and my school life. By now, Chongching was under daily bomb attacks. The rocky, hilly terrain provided natural places for bomb shelters. I remember running through the streets, clutching MaoMao, and joining the crowds of people seeking refuge in the caves. One time the missile lodged in the rocks above us and did little harm. Another time, I was in the bank during a bombing raid. We managed to get into the basement and escape, as the upper stories in the building were the only ones damaged. The rural areas outside Chongching were safer. Because of the upheaval outside and the turmoil inside, I became progressively thinner.

I longed for the war to end so that my education could continue. At last a chance came. A teaching job opened up in a Christian school in Kunming. So in the autumn of 1944, we left foggy Chongching for the sunny climate of Kunming in the far southwest.

Two months after arriving at the new school, I fell sick with pleurisy and lay in an Anglican mission hospital. We were still strangers in this city, and my daughter had to stay in our room at the school. She was 7 years old and had left behind her baby name, MaoMao. Now I called her Lansin. She went to school during the day, and in the evening teen-age students cared for her. At nighttime she slept with me, and on holidays the hospital made an exception and allowed her to stay with me.

The weeks wore on, and I was anxious to get well and return to teaching. By now I had already lost my position and my little room at the school.

Every morning I anticipated the doctor's visit and expected him to tell me I could go. One morning, the doctor came to my bed and casually asked,

"Have you been breast-feeding a baby?"

"No. Why?" I asked him."

"We have discovered some black spots on your left upper lung." he responded as he moved on to the next patient.

I was stunned. A dark curtain fell. All my ambitions and dreams disappeared like broken bubbles. There was no cure or medicine to treat tuberculosis then. This seemed like a death sentence, and I was in total despair. Could I send my daughter to my mother and end my life? But Mother lived thousands of miles away, in enemy-occupied territory. I could not even get a letter to her, so sending my daughter was out of the question. What was I to do?

That evening, Pastor Cai, the chaplain, visited the wards. He spoke as a true gentleman, with wisdom and sincerity. When he found me crying, he said, "Teacher Duan, God loves us, but we are doomed to suffer because of our sin against him. He doesn't want us to perish." His words touched me deeply. I looked at Pastor Cai, wanting to hear more. He went on,

"It says in the Bible that God loved the world so much that He gave His one and only Son to die so that everyone who believes in Him should not perish but have everlasting life." He waited, letting the words sink into my mind. Then he continued with more fervor:

"The Lord Jesus Christ came to die on the cross for our iniquities. He called us to come to Him with our heavy burden." At that moment a warm stream flooded my heart. I trembled at the thought of trusting this God of dignity, might and mercy to do what I could not do for myself. How could I refuse this invitation to come with my heavy heart? With a great feeling of release, I cast all my sins and worries on my Redeemer.

Christmas followed on the heels of my decision. It was my first experience with this holy day! Deep joy and peace reigned within me, and I gladly joined in the celebration.

The hospital stay dragged on for six months. Then, in the spring of 1945, the doctor told me to go home and rest for two more years. But I could not afford to leave. Where could I go? How could I pay my hospital bill? Even if I sold all my possessions, I still would not have enough money to cover the bill. I had no way out -- no job, no place, no money, no friends. The one thing I had, active TB, nobody wanted. For the first time I turned to my Lord and told Him my troubles.

Miracles began to happen. Miss Chao, the head nutritionist, often brought me nourishing leftovers from the special patients' trays. The chicken soup, egg, steak, noodles, or the lotus root starch always tasted good to me. One day, as I was eating the beef porridge she brought me, Miss Chao excitedly said, "Guess what! In the staff meeting yesterday they decided to grant you a subsidy."

"What?!" I asked. I did not quite understand.

"After studying your case, the hospital staff decided to utilize their fund for poor patients to pay your bill!"

I had no words. What surprise! I thanked God for His great mercy and gained faith. Soon after this, a visitor to the patient in the bed next to me learned of my plight. She offered to have us stay in a small storage room under the stairs in her house, and I had a simple, but adequate place to live. So I left that hospital without any debts, except the new one I would forever owe my Savior Jesus Christ. Now I was a member of God's family and was no longer alone.

青草地

2
Green Pastures

Therefore if anyone is in Christ, he is *a new creation; old things have passed away; behold, all things have become new.*
II Corinthians 5:17

The Lord is my shepherd; I shall not want. He makes me to lie down in green pastures; He leads me beside still waters.
Psalm 23:1 & 2

Once out of the hospital I wasted no time in attending confirmation classes and getting baptized. Pastor Chou, the head of the British Anglican Church in Kunming, led the ceremony. Pastor Tsai stood as my godfather.

Still in need of a job, I knew that a TB patient was not welcome anywhere. Pastor Tsai, however, knew four British Presbyterian missionaries transferred from Fugian Province on the southeast coast to Kunming in the far west because of the war. I had studied English for six years in high school and competed in English speech competition. The missionaries knew Fujian dialect but needed to learn Mandarin. In the process of teaching them I could practice my English. I was hired to do the job. The textbook was the Bible, so every day I had the privilege of spending four hours in it. No other job could have afforded me such a luxury!

Everything seemed new to me, and I felt relieved of my burdens. My TB no longer bothered me. I had real hope for the future and no longer struggled alone.

In the late afternoon of August 7, 1945, newspaper boys in the streets shouted, "EXTRA! EXTRA! READ ALL

11

ABOUT IT! ATOMIC BOMB DROPPED ON HIRO-
SHIMA!" It was shocking news, and we wondered what it
meant. Two days later, the same boys were shouting that
a second atomic bomb had been dropped on Nagasaki.
The Japanese Emperor surrendered. He couldn't bear to
see the massive slaughter of his people. I wondered how
conscious he was of the suffering he had caused us in
China! The Japanese withdrew completely. Our beloved
motherland, though tragically devastated, regained peace
and unity almost instantly. Mail routes returned to business as usual, so I wrote a letter to my loved ones in Jiangxi
Province. How I longed to get news of them. Soon, I received a precious letter from my sister:

"My Dearest Sister,
We were so thrilled to receive your letter from
thousands of miles away. Both mother and I could
not help letting our tears run with joy. It's been
some six years now since we had news of you.
Mother has often cried and had frequent, fitful
nights dreaming of you and MaoMao. How we
have longed for you both to come home and wan-
der no more. We were heartbroken thinking of you
living in strange places with the turmoil of war. We
want you to come home.

Father died earlier this year. Mother used her
savings for the funeral arrangements. She made a
major decision to take in the two little boys born to
Father's third and youngest wife. She is raising
them as her own. Their mother is only 30 years old.
She could not support them and has since re-
married.

I am studying in the local teacher training
school. We live close by. Mother does laundry for
some of the teachers and students. She also has a
stall selling stationery and other useful things...."

The news of Father's death grieved me. I recalled life in the 1920s when I was a little girl. Father had some formal education but was largely a self-educated man. Over the years he had been the judge for various counties in three different provinces. In those days few girls went to school. My illiterate mother wanted me to read. Important men often came to see Father to seek his advice or help. If he was not home, it was considered improper for Mother to welcome them. A young child, however, could greet them, so Mother sent me. Each time I returned with the visitor's name card and proudly announced his surname. "Let me see!" Mother took the card and pointed to the first character on it. She told me, "This character is Wong. You must remember." In this way she familiarized me with many Chinese name characters. When Father discovered that I knew some characters, he sent me to school. Every evening I brought home my textbooks and chanted the lessons aloud. Mother heard everything I read and remembered it. If Father was serving in another province Mother tried to write him. She had me repeat my lessons until she heard me say the phrase she needed; then she copied it onto her paper. In this way we helped each other. By 6th grade I read the difficult novel entitled *The Red Chamber.* I couldn't understand it, but I just swallowed it whole. I loved the wonderful poems and descriptions and must have read it more than ten times. In retrospect, I felt deeply grateful for the educational opportunities provided by my parents. And now Father was dead.

My mother and sister were obviously struggling. I understood their loving hearts, but still I did not want to let them know about my TB. We had no means of transportation anyway, so I sent them a little money I had saved and assured them I would come home someday.

Several months later, the British missionaries left Kunming for their assignments in the rural areas. My next job took me 100 miles south to Jianshui in Yunnan Province.

Four young Presbyterian missionaries, one woman from Canada and three from Australia, were to start a clinic as the first step in establishing a hospital. I was to teach them Chinese. Just before we left, a special, anonymous gift arrived in an envelope. Upon opening it, I found one hundred dollars in Chinese currency! Imagine! Thanks be to this good-hearted person and to God, who knew my need and desire to send more money to my mother.

We arrived in Jianshu just a few days before Christmas, 1945. This was my second Christmas and I was thrilled to join in the festivities. Now I knew the One whose birth was being celebrated! Daily I was getting to know more about my Savior who was so humble to be born in a manger for me.

The place was actually the old Zhuge Temple, named after a famous historical Chinese military leader. We decorated the big hall with red, silver and gold ribbons and paper lanterns. Large inscriptions and carved images praising Zhuge framed the doorways. We covered them with posters colorfully inscribed in Chinese characters: "King of Kings," "Lord of Lords," "Wonderful Savior," "Emmanuel," and "Prince of Peace." I was excited to discover that my Lord was the King of Kings, yet His love brought Him to a lowly birth.

The hymnbook caught my interest. The words linked with music entered my mind easily. Singing this way was new to me. We learned to sing "Silent Night," "Hark the Herald Angels Sing," and "The First Noel." A small pump organ rang out the hymns. Standing behind the organ, I watched with interest as Dr. Helen McKenzie played for services. She was an Australian surgeon, and she played with fervor. It was easy to pick up the melodies. The more hymns I learned to sing, the stronger my desire grew to play the organ.

In junior middle school we were taught to read music in staves and figures. Very slowly, I managed to try a simple hymn on the organ by locating the notes in the right hand, then the left. Practicing again and again, I finally played the hands together. Sometimes Dr. McKenzie corrected my mistakes. "What a Friend We Have in Jesus" was the first hymn I mastered. Hymn by hymn, my repertoire expanded. Playing the organ consumed all my spare time. In early 1947 Dr. McKenzie suggested I return to Kunming to have my lungs checked. By then I had learned 50 hymns.

The doctor ordered me to rest. I could not return to the mission in Jianshui to tutor the missionaries in Chinese so they were forced to move to Beijing to continue language school. Both McKenzie sisters brought us our things on their way to Beijing. It was difficult to say good-bye to these dear friends.

Once again I was without a job. Most schools refused to hire a TB patient, and Pastor Cai was in America. Even my newfound joy in playing the organ could not feed us. We lived in a borrowed room in the courtyard of the Chinese Presbyterian Church and entrusted our lives to the Lord Jesus.

One day in June, Pastor Chou greeted me after the Sunday service and said, "There is an Anglican branch church with a school in Dali. The warm climate would be good for you, and the cost of living is low. Perhaps you could help in some way at this mission. I will be happy to send a letter of introduction if you decide to go."

I thanked him for this information and went home to consider it and pray. We had no open doors, no chance of survival here in Kunming. But oh, how reluctant I felt to pick up and go to yet another strange place. Now was the time when I should be returning to my home in the east like everyone else displaced by the war. It didn't make sense to go even further west — further, still, from my beloved mother and sister! But I had no other way to go.

Lansin and I packed a few belongings and boarded a bus

for Dali on an early morning in July, 1947. The summer
rains had come. As I looked out the rainswept window,
my mind went back to another bus ride eight years earlier.
So much had happened since that bleak day when all my
hopes were dashed with the death of my husband. What
amazing grace! The Lord had brought me from despera-
tion to a peaceful life. I knew I could rely on Him in yet
another strange place.

"Savior, like a shepherd lead us, much we need thy
tender care" sang Lansin, now ten years old.

The sound of her voice was sweet and touched my heart,
"Yes, Lord, I'll find rest and safety in your fold," I joined
Lansin in singing, "Blessed Jesus, blessed Jesus."

Two days later we arrived at dusk in Xiaguan and were
carried by horsecart 30 miles to Dali, well known for its
marble. The oval-shaped city is located between the snow
-capped Cang Mount and the lovely, green Er Lake, which
stretches far north, paralleling the mountains.

Carrying our simple luggage, Lansin and I began walking toward the city.

"Mama, look at the clouds floating around the moun-
taintops!" exclaimed Lansin.

The sight was beautiful, indeed! Fishing boats drifted to
and fro on the lake. Life already seemed easier in this
quiet, pleasant place. We continued walking northward.
The long street was lined on both sides with shops and
table stalls selling marble vases, ink stands and screens.
Once we were inside the South Gate, I stopped at a marble
vendor's table and asked directions to the Anglican Mission School.

At the school, I met Pastor Wen and gave him Pastor
Chou's letter. As he read it, I studied this man who was
both pastor and schoolmaster in this mission. He was
dressed in casual clothes. There was a gentle firmness
about him. His forehead wrinkled in exasperation as he
folded the letter. He paused a moment and then said
thoughtfully,

"Life here is also not easy. However, since you are already here, we'll see what we can do."

"Thank you so much," I responded.

"I'm not sure where you and your daughter can stay," he continued, thinking out loud. "As you can see, there are only two buildings on this compound. Seven orphans, a Christian teacher and I live above the kindergarten building. The other building has classrooms and the staff room. The only empty room is in the attic above the school gate. You can live there."

So Lansin and I were shown our new "home," a triangular storage room. We climbed the ladder to the entry. Once inside the room, my eyes took in our surroundings. The floor was only fifteen feet long and nine feet wide. A large window faced west. At least we had a roof over our heads, but would there be anything I could do in this school? My eyes ventured past the church and school compound and found comfort in looking at Er Lake and the fishing village in the distance.

The school compound was surrounded by a stone wall. I was amazed at how they had constructed it. Huge cacti grew out of the soil wedged between stones on the sides and top of the wall. The blossoms were beautiful and the spines served as a kind of natural protective device. A pathway ran between the playing fields (playgrounds) and was lined with flowers of all kinds: camellias, red lilies, lilacs, azaleas, carnations, snapdragons and marigolds. I found out later that Pastor Wen himself worked on the gardening in his spare time. Sometimes he enlisted the help of the orphans so that he could talk with them as a father would.

After getting settled, I approached Pastor Wen and asked him if I could practice playing the organ in the church. He said there could be no problem with that and then continued, "We have no one to play the organ for our services. Would you be willing to play hymns for the church?"

"I'm just a beginner!" I responded in surprise. "But I would be willing to try."

"I don't expect perfection," he went on. "I'll let you have the hymns a week ahead of time so that you can practice. God will help you to serve Him!"

I was really pleased that I could try to do that. And those words — "to serve Him"— were new to me. To think that I could serve my heavenly Father, my merciful, mighty God! What a beautiful idea — it shed on me a brilliant light.

I thanked Pastor Wen for the opportunity. Every week I practiced three or four hymns. The words and music touched me.

After two months in Dali my health had improved. My daughter had missed several months of school due to our moving. So one afternoon I was helping her review her lessons when one of the orphans called to me from below our attic room. "Mrs. Duan, Pastor Wen wants to see you."

I hurried over to the kindergarten building. Pastor Wen greeted me: "It is good of you to come. How is your health?"

"Much improved," I responded.

"Good. I know you have some teaching experience, and our superintendent is leaving. Would you be willing to do some teaching?"

I was surprised by this request. "Thank you. I am willing to do some work here at the school. Even if the pay is not much, it is better than no job at all."

"I know you are a Christian," he said, looking at me calmly and encouragingly. Then he added, "Everything we do should be for the glory of God. I will back you as long as you are serving the Lord heartily."

Despite the fact that the school could only pay me minimum wages, I felt so enthusiastic. This job was what I had longed for.

Pastor Wen remained the headmaster and carried out the administrative duties. That fall semester I became the superintendent. We enforced a new set of strict rules for the students. I organized instruction classes to raise the level of teachers' skills. Early morning assemblies were used for moral instruction. Teachers agreed on the theme, helped prepare the assembly program and then carried out the theme in their individual classrooms throughout the day. In this way both teachers and students benefited.

Our school gained a good reputation throughout the city. The students were well disciplined and showed promise academically. People in Dali society praised our school for the moral education, as we trained students not to lie, steal, or curse. The Magistrate of Dali sent three of his children to study at our school. His wife became a good friend of mine.

December of 1947 was approaching. It was my third Christmas. There was much preparation to do. We decorated all the classrooms and church, taught the students Christmas carols and a candle dance. We also prepared a drama to act out the story of the Holy Birth of Jesus.

Over 200 people attended the celebration — including all the students, teachers, parents and church members. Pastor Wen preached the wonderful Good News about the Savior born to deliver sinners. After the service and drama, some of the students and teachers, wearing white choir robes, went caroling along the streets and to the homes of the other teachers and church members. It was so exciting for all of us!

We had 12 teachers in our school: three young men and nine young women. One of the young men named Li was a Christian from a neighboring county, living in the school.

All the others lived in their own homes. One of the young women was a Muslim. Pastor Wen led morning and evening prayers every day with the seven orphans, Li, my daughter and me, as well as Yang Sao, the young woman who helped me with cooking and washing. Sometimes Teacher Li and I would take turns leading.

Gradually, a few other teachers began to attend. By spring term of 1948, all the other teachers were coming to morning prayers. Pastor Wen taught about Jesus' sufferings, death, resurrection and ascension. His teachings had a great impact on us all. On Easter Sunday five teachers and my maid were baptized. Our Christmas joys were brighter than ever that same year because six more teachers and some 20 students were baptized.

Life was simple but good. I had almost forgotten that I had been a TB patient because I was kept busy day and night with duties in the school and church.

夫 志

3
My Vow

*"I can hear my Savior calling, I can hear my Savior calling, I
can hear my Savior calling, 'Take thy cross and follow, follow,
Me.'"*   Hymn

*"He will fulfill the desire of those who fear Him; He also will
hear their cry and save them."*   Ps. 145:19

Blessing was heaped upon blessing in Dali. After attending the Anglican church, I often attended services at
the China Inland Mission. There were quite a few missionaries at the Fuyin Gospel Hospital. I helped some of
them learn Chinese and earned a little money. Our textbook was still the Bible. Some who knew a bit of Chinese
would read the Gospels. Those who knew more of the
language would read from the Old Testament, Psalms, or
Proverbs. As I got to know these people, the dedication
to the Gospel of each one touched me deeply. I would not
be willing to come to live in a remote, backward place
like Dali, had it not been for the war. Yet they had left far
better homes to come and to suffer for the sake of the
gospel. Some of them even went to the far west, working
among the minorities. I admired such courage, sincerity
and kindness. They told me the story of Hudson Taylor
(Founder of the China Inland Mission) and his life of service to China. I was inspired and longed to have the
same dedication! Two of the pastors' wives, Judy Snow
and Mona Joyce, became intimate friends of mine.
Mona's daughter attended our school.

The hymnbook we used in the Anglican church was

"Pu Tien Song Zan" ("The Whole Universe Praises"). In Dali I learned almost all 512 hymns. The CIM hymn book "Song Zhu Sheng Ge" ("Holy Songs for Praising the Lord") contained some of my favorites: "Be Still My Soul," "Abide With Me," "O Love That Wilt Not Let Me Go," "Lead Kindly Light," and "Nearer My God to Thee." I often sang them with tears, feeling that I owed the Lord so much.

One evening, in a prayer meeting, we sang the hymn "What Hast Thou Giv'n To Me?" The chorus repeated, "I gave my life for thee, what hast thou given to Me?" My heart was deeply touched. I could not help saying in my heart, "Oh! Lord, I want to give my whole life to you." Over a period of time, through many hymns and Bible verses, Christ called me. "Come. Take your cross and follow me!" My heart burned. My soul was trembling. Never before had I been so aware of the closeness of the mighty God. I could only respond in song: "Where He leads me I will follow and go with Him, with Him all the way."

I surrendered all my life to the Lord and dedicated myself as a piece of clay into the hands of the Great Potter. Gradually, I realized how much my life had changed. In the past I climbed up the ladder of the world, trying to get somewhere high, successful and satisfactory. Now my eyes were fixed on my Savior, whose Holy Spirit had made me thirsty for Bible teachings. I was only acquainted with the Gospels and some Old Testament stories. A desire began to grow within me — someday I would study in a theological college in order to serve my Savior well. At the moment, I knew that my primary task was to help the students know the Savior.

Toward the end of 1948, Pastor Wen returned to his hometown in the far northeast. A new man, Pastor Hou, came to take his place. During the spring term of 1949, things did not go smoothly at the school. Pastor Hou had quite different views about keeping the school rules. Some of his ways of dealing with people were disappointing. I felt discouraged.

My daughter was finishing primary school. I needed to take her back to Kunming to attend a proper middle school. This move would take me a step closer to my mother and sister, too. I had many doubts. My missionary friend Mona comforted me and suggested that I wait for God's guidance.

Toward the end of spring term, without consulting anyone, Pastor Hou announced in a staff meeting that he would appoint another teacher to be superintendent. I was surprised by this unexpected decision. He said that I had too much work and he would lighten my load. My only task would be to discipline the students because, he thought, I was good at that. At that moment I understood that it was time to leave. I was glad that the teachers were better equipped now and could run the school. A good foundation had been laid. I took the news quietly and thanked God for making it clear.

I made preparations to return to Kunming in time for Lansin to take the entrance examination in July. Once again I had obstacles: I had no place to live and needed money to pay for travel expenses. I prayed and waited.

The only person I knew in Kunming was the magistrate's wife, Mrs. Lo. She had moved there a few months earlier. I wrote her a letter and felt encouraged by her response that Lansin and I could live with her if I tutored her children for the entrance examination. Our daughters would be good playmates and could study together. So one problem was settled.

For some time I had been inquiring about buses traveling to Kunming. One morning a friend of mine came to tell me, "A bus leaves for Kunming tomorrow morning. Are you ready to go?"

My head began to spin. This was the opportunity I

had awaited, but without money for the bus fare, how could we go? "I'll let you know later!" I told him.

I pleaded with God to show me how to solve this problem. There appeared to be no way we could make this bus, and we would have to wait a few days for another one. I stopped packing and made my way to Pastor Hatton's home. I had attended his English Bible Class and helped play the organ on Sunday afternoons. I thought I should tell him I was leaving.

As I walked into the Hattons' sitting room, I noticed he was counting silver coins.

"Here she is!" said Mrs. Hatton as I entered.

"I'm glad you've come!" exclaimed Mr. Hatton. "This is for you. I was to send it over to you." He handed me 60 small pieces of silver worth 30 Yuan.

Tears came to my eyes instantly. I did not know what to say to express my gratefulness to the Hattons and to God. I told them my situation.

"God laid you on our hearts," he said. "I thought you had some need."

"Oh, thank you!" I said. Words failed me. When I got home, I prayed in tears to God. The words of I Kings 17:14 came to mind: "The flour in the jar had not run short and the oil in the bottle had never run out."

After lunch I went to my friend and got the bus tickets. Then I spent the rest of the afternoon getting ready. When I went to say good-bye to Mona, I told her what had happened. "Let's praise the Lord!" she said with a smile. Opening up the hymn book, she played the small organ and we both sang,

"All the way my Savior leads me,
What have I to ask beside?"

Ever since that time this song has been the dearest melody resounding in my memory:

"This my song through endless ages,
Jesus led me all the way."

On July 1, 1949, I returned to Kunming. Lansin and I moved into Mrs. Luo's house. My time was spent job-hunting and helping Mrs. Luo's children and Lansin review for the middle school entrance examination.

On the third evening, Mrs. Luo's nephew dropped by for a visit. I could not help overhearing their family conversation. They talked about the broadcasting station where he worked.

"The station is planning to air a new program on education," remarked Mrs. Luo's nephew. They have advertised in the newspaper for some announcers to work in the Yunnan Province Education Broadcasting Station. An examination for the applicants will be held tomorrow."

Mrs. Luo turned to me and said, "Teacher Duan, this would be a good opportunity for you. I'm sure you would qualify. Why don't you try?"

I had actually been listening with great interest to their conversation and nodded in agreement. But before I could inquire further, Mrs. Luo continued talking with her nephew, "She has been the teacher of your cousins. She is talented and speaks fairly good Mandarin...."

Her nephew turned to me and said, "All right, you may come early tomorrow morning before the examination. I will get you an application and you can take the test afterward."

The next morning I joined 70 other competitors in taking the oral and written tests. In the oral examination, each of us had to announce some news, as well as recite and read something in English. Three days later the newspaper and radio announced the winners. My name topped the list. Mrs. Luo's nephew said I had done the best because I had correctly read a Chinese character which none of the other applicants recognized. Just four days before I'd had no hope of employment. Now I looked forward to starting this new job feeling both confident and competent to do the work. An old Chinese poem described this turn of events: "There seems to be no path where the mountains and rivers end. Lo! Yonder appears another village with brilliant blossoms and wispy willows."

On July 10 I joined four other announcers and began working for the station. Everything went smoothly. I admired one of the young men who took the night shifts because he was attending university during the day. It seemed like a good plan and one that I might try someday.

About this same time, Lansin and Mrs. Luo's daughters took the middle school entrance examination and passed. They were accepted at Tiannan Middle School, a Christian school located in a suburb 12 kilometers west of Kunming. They had to board at the school, and the fall term began September 1. It was urgent that I find a way to pay Lansin's tuition and boarding expenses. My job at the station could not begin to meet all these needs

I was also concerned about our living situation. Mrs. Luo had a large family and since they had just moved to Kunming recently, they were staying in temporary quarters awaiting a proper house. We were quite crowded. As soon as Lansin was settled in her boarding school, I planned to move into the dormitory at the broadcasting station.

One day while out walking in the street, I heard someone calling me from across the street, "Teacher Duan, Teacher Duan!" I turned to see who it was. It was Mrs. Bi, who had sent her sons to our boarding school in Dali.

"When did you come to Kunming? Let's go to my house and have a chat. Where is your daughter? Where do you live?" Mrs. Bi continued. I answered her questions as we walked to her house. I could see that she had a well-built, two-story house. She and her husband, a manager of a big business, and her sons were the only occupants.

She continues, "Come to live here in my house. It is not far from the broadcasting station! You are a fine person and one of the best teachers my sons ever had! We'd like to have you here. I have told my sisters all about you. They will be happy to meet you." She was so warm-hearted, and her sons also begged me to come so I could help them with their lessons. In the end I consented. She showed me a well furnished room. The big bed had springs and a mattress. I thanked her and promised to move over in a few days.

When I returned to Mrs. Luo's home, she expressed relief and happiness for me. "My husband has just been promoted to another district, so we will be leaving Kunming soon." She paused and then said, "By the way, I have some bad news for you. My nephew came by to say that the broadcasting station won't need you anymore."

"What? Why did they dismiss me?" I asked in disbelief.

"You made a mistake in your work. You read something incorrectly, and the boss heard you. It was the name of an actress in the Beijing opera. You read Mei Miaoziang. Her name is Jiang Miaoxiang. Don't you know? She is a famous star. "

It was true. The two Chinese characters Jiang and Mei are similar. I had carelessly glanced at the name and, because I was unfamiliar with this opera singer, I misread her name. I felt disappointed in myself.

But I had already been wondering if this was the right job for me. It was boring repeatedly playing music. It seemed pointless to me when I longed to go to a theological college. There was no escape. I had to work to eat and live, so I prayed earnestly that God would open a door for me. I did not feel at all confident or competent as I had the first day of work at the station. My faith faltered.

扎根

4
Taking Root

And whoever believes on Him will not be put to shame.
Romans 9:33

He shall be like a tree
  Planted by the rivers of water,
  That brings forth its fruit in its seasons,
  Whose leaf shall not wither;
And whatever he does shall prosper.
Psalm 1:3

Two weeks flew by and I remained unemployed. By this time I was no longer a stranger in Kunming. I contacted a few friends in various schools in the area. Teaching positions were all filled, however, because school would be starting in just a few days. I would have to look elsewhere for a job.

Since my return to Kunming in July, I had been attending China Inland Mission's Trinity Church. Pastor Owen and his wife had become good friends of mine. One Sunday after church, Mrs. Owen came up to me and said, "Come! Follow me to my house. Someone wants to see you!" She led me to her house behind the church and introduced me to Pastor Bromley, the school-master of the CIM Bible School. He looked very wise and gentle.

He greeted me using very good Chinese. Then he said, "We just learned about your coming from Dali. You know, our music teacher recently left for the Chongching Theological College. We need someone to take his place, and we also need a teacher of Chinese literature. We prayed that the Lord would send us someone suitable. During the prayer time, God revealed this message through His Word: 'For yet in a very little while, he who is coming will come, and will not delay.' So we thanked the Lord and waited. Then I received a letter from Pastor Hatton in Dali, talking about your looking for a chance to study the Bible. He wondered if we could help you with that desire, and he also told us what you did in Dali. In considering your case, we decided we can help one another! What would you think of teaching music and Chinese literature to two different levels and auditing Bible classes in your spare time? This one stone would kill two birds at one time."

I was thrilled! The whole situation seemed too ideal. Never could I have dreamed of something so perfect. At last I could study the Bible! So I said, "Yes! I shall be delighted to do so. Where is your school located?"

"Our school is in Chejiabi which is thirteen kilometers west of Kunming. We'll begin immediately to prepare a room for you."

"Is it in the same direction as the Tiannan Middle School?"

"Yes. We are one kilometer beyond that institution. The two schools are located on opposite sides of the same road one kilometer apart."

I was overjoyed. This meant Lansin could live with me and walk to school. She would not need to board at the school. I was too busy thinking as he continued.

"We have about 30 students and six teachers, including three foreign teachers and three Chinese teachers. We all live on the campus. Since the school charges no tuition and has no fund, all the teachers and students live by faith. The Lord has mercifully kept us going well."

"I will be very happy to follow your good example and have faith."

"Good. The fall term begins in one week. Your room

will be ready so you can move in anytime."

After I assured him that I would move in a few days prior to school beginning, he shook hands with me and said warmly, "Thank God. You are the very person to come."

His words made me feel accepted by God as well as by the staff. God had clearly prepared the way for me. When I decided to serve Him wholeheartedly, he gave me my heart's desire. What a wonderful Lord!

After this conversation, I returned to Mrs. Bi's house and found her chatting with her sisters, who had come to visit. When they heard I had found a job out of town, the older sister said, "We are happy that you have a new job, but we hate to spare you. I hope that you will come back on weekends. You and Lansin should make our house your home." I thanked them and promised that I would come as often as possible.

My mind turned to packing and preparing to leave. I had only a few days if I was going to get to the school in time to make lesson plans before the students arrived. Money was again a problem. The month's work at the radio station had kept us going, but I had no savings. The little money I had in my hand would not cover moving expenses, my daughter's tuition, books and school supplies. I did not know what to do nor how to answer my daughter's frequent question: "Ma! What are you going to do for my tuition? And even if the school lets us pay a little at a time, how will I buy my books?" All I could reply was, "We'll pray. God will provide."

On the morning of August 28, 1949, I awoke early but remained in bed wondering what to do. The minutes ticked away. I was restless and ready to go but had no alternative. The Luos had already done so much for me. I couldn't ask them for help.

My deep thoughts were interrupted by a voice: "Ma! Aren't we going to the school today? The others have all registered long ago." Lansin had just awakened and these were the first words out of her mouth .

"I've been thinking that we should go and talk to the school officials today," I said as I dragged myself out of bed.

Just then, there was a knock on the door. I opened it. There stood Mrs. Bi and her sister. I welcomed them. After we had greeted one another, Mrs. Bi took the piece of red floral fabric in her hand and spread it out on the bed. "Lansin, do you like it? Let your mother make a new dress for you to wear to school!"

Then Mrs. Wong stepped forward and handed me 30 silver coins. "I intended to buy something for you," she said. "But then I thought it better for you to buy something to please YOUR heart!"

I thanked them heartily. As they stepped out the door they again assured us that we would always be welcomed in their home on weekends and that my services as tutor might also be needed by Mrs. Bi's sons.

After closing the door, I turned and looked at Lansin. I could see the sparkles of happiness in her eyes. I said, "Surely, the Lord is always watching and caring. We must praise and thank Him and trust Him wholeheartedly."

The next morning Mrs. Bi and Mrs. Wong met us at the West Gate of Kunming to bid us farewell. As we climbed into the horsecart, they repeated their good-byes and the reminder, "Come back often!"

The driver shouted, "Giddyup!" The cart lurched forward. I waved to our dear friends and thought how good it was to know that we would always be welcomed by them. The horses ran westward along the main highway out of Kunming. We were surrounded by people coming and going on foot, in cars, and on bicycles. Even though the horsecart jostled us from side to side, the ride in the open air afforded us a clear view of the surrounding

fields. In the autumn the sky seemed so high and the atmosphere was so fresh. Sitting beside me, Lansin began
to sing a song we had often sung in Dali:

"This is my Father's world,
And to my listening ears,
All nature sings and 'round me rings,
The music of the spheres."

It was a pleasant ride as we left the city behind and
drove toward the famous Mount West in the distance.
As I drank in the morning air, I admired the creation of
Almighty God and marveled at my Creator's merciful
care for us. To think, I had once accused Him of playing a
trick on me!

The trip took just over two hours. We rode past Lansin's new school, located on the slope of the hill. One
more kilometer brought us to the village of Chejiabi. Not
far away Lake Dian seemed to meet Mount West, also
known as Sleeping Beauty. The blue of the sky and the
white of the clouds formed a lovely backdrop for this
scene. There was the side profile of Sleeping Beauty lying
on her back with her long, beautiful hair flowing down
into Dian Lake. Perhaps this was the place where she
washed her hair!

Chejiabi was a long, narrow village on the east side of
the road, which was lined with small shops and cafes. As
soon as we disembarked from the horsecart, we spotted a
one-room house with a cross on the roof. It was a street
chapel, but nobody was there. We made our way along
the path in front of the chapel and several cottages, then
turned down toward the Bible school. It comprised two
rows of one-story houses on a slight slope, all facing
south to the lake located a half-mile away.

"Teacher Duan! Teacher Duan is here!" Some students
ran to help us carry our bags. Almost everyone, teachers
and students alike, came to welcome us. It was like coming home though we had never met these people before

nor had we ever been in this place.

We were led to a one-level house with four rooms, which we were to share with Miss Lang, a Canadian teacher. The largest room was her study, which we could jointly use as a sitting room and a place to meet with students. I was amazed to see that Miss Lang had taken the smallest room for her bedroom and had left the other two larger rooms for Lansin and me. My room was furnished with a bed, desk and dresser and was bright, neat and simple. For the first time in my wandering life, I had privacy — a quiet place where I could study and prepare lessons. I was touched when told that Pastor Bromley himself had just put a fresh coat of paint on the dresser. Lansin was excited to have a room of her own. They told us that we could eat our meals with the Bible students. That would make our lives easier and more economical. The Bible school in Chejiabi promised to be the best living situation we had ever had!

That afternoon, after unpacking, Lansin and I walked twenty minutes to her school to register. Mrs. Wong's gift had provided money for moving and for buying necessities, Lansin's books, and school supplies. The school agreed to let us pay tuition later in the term.

The fall term began on September 1, and I was full of faith and enthusiastic to embrace the work. My assignments included teaching two different levels of Chinese literature as well as music to the entire school. I also took my turn leading morning and evening prayers. Some afternoons were spent helping students make visual aids for Sunday school work. In my spare time, I attended Bible classes. To think! I could have been trapped in the radio station playing one record after another. Instead, I had a challenging and interesting life.

At Chejiabi, I felt like I had come "home" at last. The serene location by the lake and the congenial spirit among staff and students were most inviting. There seemed to be no room for sadness or grumbling here despite the fact that both staff and students lived by faith. Instead, the Spartan-like existence lent itself to positive attitudes, spiritual growth and great resourcefulness. We ate simple food such as porridge with either peanuts or pickles every day for breakfast. After standing to sing the grace, we ate heartily and found the plainest food tasty because we were hungry. Students and teachers did without things or contrived ingenious substitutes. Da Yang, a cheerful young man and president of the student body, cut off the tops of his socks to use as washcloths. In this way he literally made each sock go "the extra mile." We had no money to purchase time-saving devices such as a mimeograph machine or even silk screening apparatus, to print copies of instructional materials for the students. Of course, the Bible teachers had no need to-make copies since each student had a Bible. But my subjects, Chinese literature and music, had no texts, so the students relied on me to print copies of the materials to be studied. Pastor Bromley demonstrated a primitive, but effective, method. To print a page of music or a literature text required a hand-tool to carve away the waxy layer on the stencil paper, leaving tiny holes in the shape of the letter or the note. After ink had been brushed evenly on a piece of plate glass, the stencil paper was placed face down on the inky glass, covered with a piece of plain white paper and pressed by hand. This tedious process took about two hours of time, from carving the page of music or text to printing the 30 copies required for the students.

All my waking hours were absorbed in mothering, teaching, studying and ministering. For the literature classes, I searched modern and ancient Chinese literature to select appropriate texts to print for the students to read and study, and also instructed them in writing compositions and presenting speeches. One-fourth of the students were from minority tribes in Yunan Province and needed help with the Mandarin language. But their gift in singing was an asset to the music classes. As the school's music instructor, I selected hymns, printed them, practiced accompaniments, taught the students to read musical notation, and tutored some students on the organ. After they learned to sing parts, their skills were sharpened in duets and quartets. Before long, the choir was singing more complex pieces. We were often asked to sing for Sunday services and other special occasions. During a part of each day, I moved from the front of the class as instructor and sat in a student's desk to learn from Exodus, St. Paul's letters, or Bible geography. These classes challenged me and required squeezing out some time to study for exams.

Sundays afforded us a change of scenery and opportunities to exercise our legs, as well as our newly acquired knowledge, in outreach to surrounding villages. The students divided into teams of two and walked up to two hours away to reach fishing villages along the lake or in the hills. Each Sunday, Lansin and I joined a different team to minister in a village. In this way we rotated through all the teams and visited every locality in four months. Struck by the simplicity and sincerity of the rural people, I was particularly drawn to the lovely people in Huahongyuan village. We frequently returned there to minister.

On Sunday evenings we gathered to report what happened in the various villages that day. This evaluation time provided a means to fine-tune the ministry and to plan for the future. We always closed in prayer, entrusting the seed of the gospel into God's mighty hand.

There was no doubt that life in Chejiabi agreed with me. In fact, my friends in Kunming noticed a remarkable change. They said I wore a healthy glow and looked like a different woman! Life was too busy to think about the

TB. Preparations for Bible classes, prayer meetings, and church services were instructive and inspiring. Though my material existence was hard, the spiritual life was supported richly.

Lansin and I had many experiences which demonstrated God's faithfulness. It was a little after five o'clock one evening in early December 1949. The sun had set behind Mount West, silhouetting Sleeping Beauty's features against a colorful sky. Darkness fell quickly as Lansin returned from school. My mother's heart sensed her pensiveness. After supper, we went to evening prayers. Pastor Bromley, the American schoolmaster, was not with us. His wife announced that he had biked to Kunming on errands and was delayed. She was concerned about his riding the 13 kilometers home in the dark.

After the prayer meeting, we walked out into the night air. The new quarter moon glowed in the sky. I was thinking how helpful this moonlight would be for Pastor Bromley when Lansin broke in.

"Ma! The teacher told me that my tuition is due tomorrow. I am not to return to school without money. Have you been paid recently?"

So this was the reason behind Lansin's moodiness! The truth was that I had no money, and now I had no words for my daughter. Understanding my silence, she began to cry bitterly. "Can't you find a way? Can't you do something!?" Pain pierced my heart as I walked over and put a hand on her shoulder. "Let's pray," I whispered. "Our dear Heavenly Father will take care of everything for us just like in the old days."

We knelt together and pleaded with God to have mercy on us. I recalled His promise to be a father to the fatherless.

Afterward, I tried to comfort Lansin and told her I might borrow money from Mrs. Chu to pay for a horse-cart ride to Kunming to consult friends there. Gradually, she quieted down, finished her homework, and went to bed, still sobbing in her dreams. I knelt beside her bed and prayed once again, "Oh, Lord, have pity on us."

With no energy or heart to make lesson plans, I returned to my room and dropped into the chair. Picking up my Bible, I read Scriptures and prayed in an effort to ward off my worst fears. The compound was very quiet with only an occasional dog barking or cricket chirping. Footsteps in the passageway and a knock on my door broke the silence about 10 p.m. I opened the door. There stood Pastor Bromley, still wearing his overcoat and holding a letter in his hand.

"Sorry to disturb you, Teacher Duan!" he said. "I saw your light, so decided to bring this letter to you. A complete stranger handed it to me this afternoon and requested that I deliver it to you. You may find out the name when you open the card. Anyway, I'm off to supper. Good-night."

Baffled, I looked at the envelope with my name scrawled across it in an unfamiliar handwriting. I opened the letter at once and pulled out fifty dollars and a short note: "I admire your courage and struggle through life. I hope you find this small gift of some use. Yours in Christ." There was no name or clue as to the sender. To this day, I do not know who surprised us with this gift! I knelt down yet once more that night and tearfully thanked my Merciful and Mighty God.

The next morning Lansin awoke earlier than usual and came to my doorway. "Ma, aren't you up yet?"

"Look. God has provided your tuition!" I held out the envelope to her. With wide-open eyes she walked over and took the envelope in astonishment.

"What is this? Where did it come from?"

"Pastor Bromley brought it from Kunming. Someone in Kunming asked him to deliver it to us."

"Who?"

"I don't know. Neither does the pastor."

Lansin counted the banknotes. "Fifty! The tuition is only forty. Oh, I thank my Heavenly Father!"

"That is why I'm thinking of buying you a new dress also."

"But Ma, I need a drawing compass. I never told you because I knew you had no money. I borrowed one from a classmate, but it was very inconvenient!"

"All right. We'll get you one of your very own. Now get ready for school."

She bounced out of the room singing, "Blessed Jesus! Blessed Jesus."

Not only did I see God's hand of provision that year. I also witnessed His blessings on my music classes. People's expectations rose with the Chejiabi choir's achievements. By the fall of 1949, everyone was suggesting that we sing the "Hallelujah Chorus" Although I knew the story of Handel, I had never heard his most famous piece. I borrowed a Chinese copy from Mrs. Bromley and carefully went over the melody. As the different parts blended and played in my mind, I was awestruck. Never had I seen or heard music like this. I remembered a powerful patriotic song which grew out of the Anti-Japanese War of the thirties. A bass solo began by singing: "Who are the masters of the beautiful rivers and mountains of China?" Then the full choir in four parts replied, "We four hundred million people from the same womb!" The piece went on: "Homes can be broken, but the country should be sustained. The body may be killed, but the will must never bend." I loved this music by Huang Zi, but it was nothing compared to this composition by Handel! I transcribed it into numbered musical notation and used the primitive method to print copies for the students. Then I began to teach them their parts. Having never had formal training as a conductor, I acquired skill during choir practices. My style was not smooth, but the beats were correct. God seemed to have given me a feel for the rhythm and just enough training to be of use to Him. I did not feel equal to the task but decided just to do it for God's glory, and He would help me accomplish the impossible. Mrs. Owen, from Trinity Church in Kunming, agreed to accompany us. She came out to the Bible school twice for practice sessions. The students' excitement and inspiration grew as they prepared. I observed that they were not merely practicing to perform well. The music seemed to motivate them to dig deeper into the Scriptures. As I watched their faith deepening, I could only agree with Martin Luther, who said, "besides theology, music is the only art capable of affording peace and joy of the heart."

On Christmas Eve we traveled to Kunming and slept in Trinity Church, where we were slated to perform at 9 a.m. on Christmas Day. The entire experience, including the trip into the city and singing before large congregations, promised to be a special treat for these students. Trinity Church allowed us to stay in the guest rooms above the chapel. As we gathered for evening prayers, the air was electric with excitement. Testimonies spilled out one after another. A kind of closeness settled over us as we talked and prayed into the early morning hours. The Spirit of Christ visited us in that upper room, and, like the disciples of old, we found our hearts burning within us.

Christmas Day dawned and the doors of China Inland Mission's Trinity Church swung open. People of all types had come. Some tribal people had walked for a day or two in bare feet, wearing only a wrapped cloth, just to be present on this special day. The capacity crowd of over 700 stood as we sang Handel's chorus. Later that morning we performed before a wealthier congregation of people at St. John's Anglican Church. Even though the church was not filled, the students sang with enthusiasm and satisfied hearts, thus crowning the already powerful piece with personal passion and joy.

As Lansin and I walked out of St. John's, I heard a voice calling my full name — something I had not heard since middle school. Turning around, I saw Liuying, one of my classmates from Nanjing.

"Hi. I saw you conducting the choir. It was wonderful. You're just as active as you were at school!"

"Liuying! When did you come to Kunming? Do you usually worship here?"

"Sometimes. Come along home! Is this your daughter? We've got to catch up on all the news."

We walked to Liuying's home and met her husband and three children. She told me about her oldest son, who had been a bright, happy child until the age of 20 months when he contracted meningitis. Because they were fleeing the Japanese troops, they could not get medical attention in time. He was now ten years old but had the mind of a two-year-old.

"This is the most distressful thing in my life." she said, choking back the tears.

I could see that she was depressed, so I told her my own tragic story of losing my husband. She listened and seemed comforted. What a memorable Christmas this had been! The intimate fellowship with the students on Christmas Eve, the fine performances of Handel's great music, and this precious reunion made it my best Christmas yet.

In the spring of 1950, our choir received an invitation to perform at the traditional Chinese Spring Festival, a great event at Zion Church in Kunming. This large, red brick edifice, built by the Methodists in the early part of this century, seated at least 1,000 if every pew and aisle were packed. I knew that the spring festival would draw a crowd, so I chose a complicated piece called "Glorious!" We arrived at the church at 6:30 p.m. and walked through the large gate leading to the steps of the church. We had only 30 minutes before our scheduled performance. I immediately scanned the congregation for Mrs. Owen, our accompanist. Just then, a woman walked up and told me that Mrs. Owen would be unable to come. This news sent me reeling. Who could possibly play for us on such short notice? I only knew a few other pianists in the entire city, and it was too late to contact them. The students urged me to let them sing a cappella, but that was a risk we were not ready to take. In my heart I prayed,

O Lord, you know we want to sing for you. Show us your glory even as we sing about it tonight!

I got up and walked toward the piano. The church was so crowded that a group of young men were sitting on the floor beside the piano. There, sitting in the group, was Fu Cong, a young member of St. John's Church. I knew he was a high school student who played very well. Overjoyed, I went and asked him if he would be willing to try and accompany us. He smiled and nodded. Without so much as even a look at the music, he stood, casually placed the music on the piano and went on chatting with his friends. I was dumfounded. How would he manage without even looking at the piece in advance? I braced myself for impending disaster! When the moment came, I stood before the choir, raised the baton, looked at Fu Cong, and he began to play the introduction. We were off and running. To my surprise, his accompaniment was flawless. Afterward, I thanked him sincerely, and he smiled cordially. Some 20 years later, I read in the newspaper that he had become a world famous pianist. I could not help but smile, remembering the night God arranged for him to accompany our choir for His glory.

Part II
Being Refined
磨　煉

Orchid

Pure and elegant, with subtle fragrance,
growing in the remote valleys and
hidden rock crevices, away from worldly cares.

鉅變

5
Radical Change

This decision is by the decree of the watchers, And the sentence by the word of the holy ones. In order that the living may know that the Most High rules in the kingdom of men. Gives it to whomever He will, and sets over it the lowest of men.
                                                    Daniel 4:17

And I will bring the blind by a way that they did not know; I will lead them in paths that they have not known. I will make darkness light before them, and crooked places straight. These things will I do for them, And not forsake them..
                                                    Isaiah 42:16

In January 1950, Pastor Chu, the Chinese principal of the Bible school, returned from a preaching tour in west Yunnan Province just in time for spring term. With great enthusiasm, the students plunged into his classes on the Prophets, Paul's letters, and the Epistle to the Hebrews. Their efforts, combined with the work of the Holy Spirit, resulted in evident spiritual maturity. Clearly, the winds of the Spirit were blowing. A freshness marked the students' lives, ministries and even their singing. We were all, staff and students alike, intent on leading devoted lives and God's blessing was evident.

Kunming's mild climate has been described as "spring year-round." April's weather is the finest of all, with bright flowers, mild temperatures and gentle breezes. One lovely Sunday morning in April, we all began our customary preparations to go out to the different villages to preach. The day looked fair and one could only echo the poet's words: "God is in heaven and all is right with the world." Some students had already departed to walk long distances while others of us did not need to leave until 8 a.m.

Suddenly, two Miao students came running into the compound, shouting,

"Martial Law! Martial Law! The highway is impassable!"

"What?"

"What's happening?"

"We don't know. We went to Magai town but could not pass. Armed soldiers guarding the road refused to allow people or vehicles to proceed!"

"Where is Da Yang's group? They left before 7 a.m."

Just then another group of students came running in from a different direction.

"We reached Gaoqiao but could not pass. Da Yang's group went through the field on foot paths. The soldiers are only on the highway, not on the paths or in villages."

"Has anyone heard the news?"

"We overheard people along the road saying that Yunnan Province is having a peaceful liberation."

"A peaceful liberation? What could that possibly mean?"

The cluster of people was growing. Everyone was talking at once when Pastor Chu, with his seven-year-old son in tow, hurriedly crossed the compound to us. "Please go to the large classroom for a general meeting." he asked.

The air was charged with fear and questions as Pastor Chu began to speak.

"We cannot get much news from the liberated areas since we are under the National Government's control. What I do know is that one year ago the People's Liberation Army crossed the Yangtze River and liberated Nanjing, Shanghai, and many other cities. Throughout this past year, they have won widely in southern China. On

October 1 last year, Mao Ze-Dong, Zhou En-Lai, Liu
Shao-Qi, and others proclaimed the establishment of the
People's Republic of China in Tiananmen Square in Beijing. Recently, they have liberated our neighbor provinces
Guizhou and Sichuan. The head official of Yunnan Province decided to proclaim the adherence of our province
to Beijing in order to avoid bloodshed. That is why it is
called a peaceful liberation. After 38 years in power, the
National Government of the Republic of China has been
forced to Taiwan. We will not go out to the villages today. The situation is not clear. If, in fact, we now have a
new country with a new system, we have much to learn."

Pastor Chu closed this meeting in prayer. A general
hubbub rose as the students excitedly left the room. I was
stunned. For better or for worse, our life in the Bible
school had had little contact with the outside world.
Now, I was wondering what would happen next.

During the weeks to come, life continued at the Bible
school much as it always had. I spent one Sunday with
Liuying and she and her family were helpful in informing me about the political situation. Gradually, we
began to hear more and more about the radical change
afoot in the country. First came the movement to sup-
press counter revolutionaries followed by the movement
of land reform. Many counter-revolutionaries, were sentenced to be shot to death. Accused of exploiting the
workers, landlords and rich farmers were killed in ac-
cusation meetings, while others were driven out of their
homes to labor in order to live. None of this greatly affected the Bible school, since none of us fell into any of
these categories. We found it hard to accept this sort of
pitiful death. Besides, we were still naive in regard to
these matters and had not yet acquired the perspective of
viewing all peoples divided into classes.

One evening late in May, a staff meeting was called.
Pastor Bromley informed us that the new government

had instructed all missionaries to leave the country immediately. Prior to their departure, they were to submit personal biographies written in Chinese. This task would be too difficult even for those missionaries fluent in Chinese, so he asked me to translate them from English into Chinese. I was glad to help. Gradually, all the CIM missionaries gathered in Kunming to write their biographies and to be investigated by the government before leaving the country. I helped translate about a dozen biographies and enjoyed fellowship with old friends like Judy Snow and Mona Joyce. Lansin and I spent the summer living among the people in Huahongyuan village. The location in the hills made it a pleasant place to escape the heat. I had my first taste of leading people to a knowledge of Jesus Christ.

The missionaries left in September just before our National Day. They left me no address. I was puzzled by this, but I believed there must be good reasons for it. Anyway, being in Christ, we could pray for one another. I felt somewhat sad to see them go, but I felt optimistic about the future.

On October 1, 1950, the first anniversary of the founding of the People's Republic of China, there was a mammoth parade in Kunming. It was declared the National Day and parades were held in all the cities of China. For the first time, teachers and students of the Bible school joined. I played the accordion as our group walked through the street. It was an exhilarating experience, and we all felt new pride in our country.

In 1951, the political developments gradually affected every citizen in China. The Ministry of United Front Affairs organized all the leaders, workers and some influential church members into groups to study politics and policies in Kunming three days a week. All schools, hospitals, factories and even neighborhoods had these meetings to raise political and class consciousness through lectures on national and international affairs. We were very glad to have an opportunity to meet with many Christian friends. I saw a friend of mine, Mrs. Zhong. Her frank and open personality made her popular in Christian circles. She was a member of the Presbyterian Church and was a teacher in Kunming Medical School. It soon proved expensive and inconvenient to travel between Chejiabi and Kunming, so I did the prudent thing and moved in with Liuying and her family. In searching for a church home, I was drawn to Watchman Nee's Little Flock Church. The Bible teachers were outstanding — especially old Brother Chen. I felt like I had moved up into spiritual "higher education."

In the political meetings, we were directed to concentrate on the Three-Self Patriotic Movement. The party's policy focused on Protestant and Catholic churches, where missionaries had been involved. It required the church to be free of foreign influence and to be self-governing, self-supporting and self-propagating. There seemed to be wisdom in the direction the government was taking us. Since we were one in Christ, it only made sense to remove denominational barriers and become one large, ecumenical body. The Bible school at Chejiabi had many Bible students and a small campus west of Kunming. We were asked to join ranks and move to the Pentecost Bible School. It had a large campus in the east suburb and only eight students. The headmasters would share the administrative duties. Just before fall term the staff and students at Chejiabi locked the doors and shuttered the windows. I feasted my eyes one last time on Mount West — studying the features of Sleeping Beauty letting her hair cascade into lovely Lake Dian. The Lord had solidified my faith in this place and had allowed me to taste working for the Kingdom. With bittersweet feelings, I boarded the truck. Lansin would begin attending boarding school and return home only on weekends.

After moving, we threw ourselves into getting the newly merged Bible school on its feet and into learning the new government policies. "Labor to eat" was the way of the new society. It seemed in agreement with II Thessalonians 3:10: "If a man will not work, he shall not eat." The school started a dairy farm as a capital project. The staff and students invested money and worked in various roles. My job was sealing the bottles, arranging the students to deliver the milk and keeping the accounts. I knew nothing of cost accounting, but everyone agreed I was the person to do it. Desperate for help, I took two courses at the Evening Accounting School and did so well that they asked me to start teaching evening classes there. Every day included juggling classes at the Bible school, tasks at the dairy farm, political meetings and teaching accounting classes. Because of inexperience and despite our best efforts, the dairy farm failed in 1952. The two heads of the school were heavily involved in political meetings. This financial crisis meant that all the students and teachers were suffering. I was grateful for my job at the accounting school, and supplemented my income by knitting and sewing. I thought my new life should please the government's call for production.

By the spring of 1953, another nationwide movement swept the country. The San Fan ("three against") movement was opposed to corruption, waste and bureaucracy within the government, the military and large institutions. Everyone was potentially guilty in some aspect. The workers fought against the factory owners, students fought against teachers, and the masses turned against the employers. Factories, government institutions, hospitals and schools could not maintain schedules and were paralyzed. Special conditions were placed on the churches. All missionaries were considered imperialists since the privilege of doing mission work was accorded by the Nanjing Unequal Treaty, which concluded the Opium War, a war we had lost, in 1842. The missionary movement was considered an invasion, with the missionaries being spies. Caught in the mood of the whole society, church members, workers, and Bible students were mobilized to inform against their pastors, teachers and administrators. Everyone was encouraged to spy on one another. Spring semester of 1953 at the Bible school never got under way.

As the movement went deeper, more offenders were "dug out." Rich homes were looted and some capitalists committed suicide. Church leaders had to confess offenses and relationships with foreign missions. I found it hard to adjust my way of thinking. One cool mid-fall morning in a study meeting, an official announced:

"The counter-revolutionary Chen Ruo-Tian is under arrest. Forty years ago he was the head of the security bureau in his home-town."

Old Brother Chen?! He was the most respected church leader in the area. By singling him out, the authorities were succeeding in "beating down" the rest of us. My head and heart were spinning. I looked around the room. Others registered confusion but none of us dared ask questions. The gaps between us seemed to be widening. We were becoming islands. There could be no discussion with old friends.

Some days later at a general meeting, several study groups joined forces. The attendees included pastors, elders, Bible school teachers, and lay leaders. At this meeting, the political leader urged us to abandon Brother Chen.

We were all facing a crucial test. How could we be honest witnesses? I watched and listened as faithful friends put on different faces and betrayed their brother. Even his wife had to call him a counter-revolutionary and showed her stand against him. After the meeting, the political leader approached me and said,

"You, Teacher Duan, you know something. Tell us your secrets. You knew this man. It's your chance to speak out. You better do so at the next meeting!" A bitter battle raged in my heart. What could I say? I refused to fabricate the stories they wanted to hear. I could not find anything to prove him a counter-revolutionary and I had no secrets to keep.

Soon after this meeting, all the outstanding pastors, including our two heads of the Bible school, were isolated for forced introspection and confession. Without the shepherds, the sheep were scattered. On one occasion, word was sent out to all church members and Christians to gather at Zion Church on a certain evening. As I entered this great church, I remembered the festival three years earlier when our choir had sung to the glory of God, accompanied by a young, talented stranger. Now the church hosted a different crowd. Packed with mostly Christians, churchgoers, as well as some government officials, the atmosphere was charged with fear and suspicion. Preceded by loud drum rolls and shouts, party zealots pushed Li Bai-Ren to the center-stage for questioning and accusations. He had been to Taiwan and was once the head of the Rotary Club. This dear Christian brother stood there as activists in the crowd shouted:

"Shoot him to death! He is a stubborn counter-revolutionary!"

One woman, the wife of a gateman and a non-Christian, turned and snarled at me as she yelled accusations. She relished the opportunity to insult the educated people as well as the Christians. There was nothing to say. This was too much for me. My heart kept missing beats.

By the end of 1954, the movement had ground to a halt. Nearly all the pastors who had been mainstays in various churches were imprisoned or sent to labor camps. Only one pastor remained in Kunming. A capable graduate of the North China Theological College, he became the chairman of the Three-self Patriotic Movement Committee of Kunming. He gained popularity with the authorities by informing them about other church leaders and pastors. While these people served terms in prisons or labor farms, he prided himself in being head pastor of Trinity Church. He and his family occupied the very rooms above the chapel where the choir and I stayed on Christmas Eve in 1949. Our hearts had burned within us on that night 17 years before as the Spirit moved. But in 1967 a different kind of fire swept through those upper rooms, killing the pastor and his family.

In the early summer of 1953, I was teaching in the Evening Accounting School and attending the daily political study meetings. Every morning, about 40 to 50 of us met for four hours (from 8 -12 a.m.) in the YMCA. The government, the Religious Affairs Bureau staff officials, presented a new policy and then most of the time was used in open discussion. It was at one of these meetings that my friend Mrs. Zhong told me she had reommended me for a teaching position in physics at the Provincial Public Health School. I was surprised since I only had a high school diploma myself. But she had been so pleased with my tutoring her children in math and physics that she felt confident I could do it. After looking at the textbooks, directly translated from the ones used in the Soviet Union, I agreed to take the job. They offered me a temporary contract which meant the salary was reasonable but there were no benefits.

Beginning with the fall term of 1953, I started teaching eight hours of physics a week at the Kunming Public Health School in addition to the accounting classes. It took me two hours to walk to and from my place at the accounting school in the south of Kunming to the health school in the north of the city. Because political meetings took up my mornings, there was little time to make lesson plans, so I would find myself knitting and figuring out physics lessons while walking the two hours between schools. In my spare time I audited teacher-training courses and borrowed instruments for student experiments (from the teacher-training college) since our newly established school was short of lab equipment. I also played the organ at all church services and taught Sunday school. My life was so full that I found myself walking quickly everywhere so as to make up time.

By the fall of 1955, I was transferred to a newly established nursing school where I was to teach mathematics. I loved teaching math so this pleased me very much. I moved in with my old friend Mrs. Wong and took the bus to school. Soon after the new term had begun, I was put in charge of extracurricular activities for the entire school. I organized all 500 students into clubs such as choir, poetry, dance, Beijing Opera, Yunnan Opera, comic dialogue, band, drama, drawing and painting. I invited other teachers to help coach the groups and organize performances. It was a great success.

By the end of the school year, the principal did not hesitate to assign me new tasks. I gladly consented to add teaching Chinese literature to my already busy schedule come the new fall term. Though other teachers were college graduates and more qualified, still I found myself more and more in demand. With all this work and attention, it only seemed fair that I should receive tenure and be granted the position of a state cadre, an officially appointed teacher with all the benefits. This became my goal.

God had given me talents and it seemed appropriate and patriotic to contribute my talents to our new country. Though not conscious of it, I had become a person with a dual personality. I behaved as a good Christian but was competing in a worldly race.

菅 敎

6
God's Discipline

Yea, though I walk through the valley of the shadow of death, I will fear no evil; For you are with me; Your rod and your staff, they comfort me.   Psalm 23:4

Twenty long years had lapsed since I had seen my mother and sister. Lansin, now attending Kunming Technical College, had never met them. Surprisingly, opportunity knocked first at her door. In the autumn of 1956, she represented her college as a baseball pitcher and basketball forward at the College National Games. En route to the competition, she passed through Nanchang. She, her grandmother and her aunt met briefly on the train platform during a layover at the station. My mother and sister recognized her from photos I had sent over the years. What a precious reunion! Lansin urged my mother to visit us the following spring.

In March of 1957, Mother came. The memory remains crystal clear. We expected her to arrive by train the following day, and I had gone to a nearby theater to see a play. Walking home afterward, the lines and scenes in the drama absorbed my thoughts. I barely noticed the drizzling rain and city life around me. When I reached my street, the sound of rickshaw wheels on wet pavement drew my attention to the road. With the hood pulled down and the oil cloth screen pulled up for protection from inclement weather, the passenger was mostly invisible. I gave little heed until I heard my name.

"Zhi-Dao!"

There sat Mother! Her familiar voice sounded strong

and high-spirited as ever. I stepped over to the rickshaw and helped her out. Twenty years melted into a moment. The sadness and suffering had carved deep wrinkles into her face. To me, she looked so good. Even for all the 60 years. That first night we chattered into the wee hours of the morning like two schoolgirls.

On weekdays I taught school and mother busied herself. On Sundays we attended Trinity Church. Afterward, Lansin and I took her sightseeing.

At this same time, Chairman Mao had called the people of China "to let a hundred flowers bloom and a hundred schools of thought contend." Meetings throughout the country provided platforms for people to air their views freely. Daily newspapers carried criticisms of the government, the Communist Party, and high officials. In our school, the teachers were divided into groups to discuss political issues. I echoed the perspectives held by others, including many outstanding professors: "Non-professionals should not exercise leadership over professionals." A common phenomenon since liberation had been the takeover of leadership in all factories, government offices, military organizations, hospitals, schools and agricultural cooperatives by Party members who had little education.

Toward the end of spring term 1957, a shocking headline appeared in bold letters in all newspapers: "THE WORKING CLASS SPEAKS--WE WON'T ALLOW THE RIGHTIST BOURGEOISIE (Capitalist Class) DESPERATELY ATTACKING OUR PARTY." The article pointed out that rightists attacked the Party by speaking their views. From that point on, the wind shifted 180 degrees. All criticism of the Party disappeared and known dissidents were singled out as capitalist rightists.

The shift had an impact on our school almost immediately. The political meetings (called "helping" meetings) switched from criticism of the government to questioning people like myself. Clearly, I was the target and the other teachers in the group came well-prepared to interrogate me. Though they still addressed me as "Teacher," they refused to listen to my explanations. Gradually, my position as a counter-revolutionary was established because of my being raised in the old society and educated in Western mission schools. During final examination week, these meetings continued. Ironically, at the same time my long-awaited ID card arrived, confirming my approved status as an official secondary technical teacher.

Summer vacation brought more frequent "helping" meetings. By this time, all titles of respect were dropped. I was no longer addressed as Teacher Duan or Comrade Duan. Now they called me by my name only. Needing to fill their quota, the zealous leaders accused 5% of the staff of being "capital rightists."

When fall term began, the classroom remained closed to me. My daily task became washing vegetables in the kitchen. The other "rightist" teachers also worked in the kitchen, but speaking to one another was strictly forbidden. Each evening we attended political meetings where the accusations grew sharper:

"What was your motive in talking about being leaders?"

"I read it in a Russian magazine. It said the highest organ of school power is the meeting of all the teachers in secondary schools in the Soviet Union. I think that should be our model as well," I responded. They furiously refused my defense and ultimately allowed no time between questions for me to make any kind of explanation. My tormenters shot questions at me in rapid-fire succession.

"Do you want to organize a reactionary group under this guise to carry out your political agenda?"

"What was your relationship with the imperialist missionaries, anyway?"

"Weren't they wrapped in the cloak of religion?"

"They are spies. You are too. You were their 'gopher.'"

"What are you doing in the Little Flock Church?"

"They are a reactionary secret society."

"You are one of them."

"Your husband was a counter-revolutionary military official of the National Party."

"He was a member of a spy organization. You are a spy!"

"How many secret meetings have you held?"

"Who are the members?"

"What is your political agenda?"

How could I untangle their twisted accusations? There was no way to straighten things out. Oh, God! What will this lead to?

"You must listen!"

"You must not be obstinate to death!"

"Make a clean break with your past for the sake of your future, your daughter and mother!"

"Remember!   TAN-BAI-CONGKUAN,   KANG-JU-CONGYAN." ("Leniency to those who confess their crimes and severity to those who refuse to confess.")

What logic! Suffocating under this unreasonable hostility, I literally found it hard to breathe. This was a fiery trial. Mother reflected my pain in her countenance and would attempt to cheer me up. If I so much as responded to her with a chuckle, those people guarding my door would push it open without a knock and chide me to consider confessing my crimes. The potential for evil in the depths of human hearts astounded me. Wild suspicion, jealousy, hatred and ignorance flourished. Insurmountable walls rose between people. Finally, Mother's heart broke, and her tears intensified my pain. Why should she bear such burdens at age sixty? She could not totally understand my ways of thinking and living. Besides, the political zealots had ways of gathering information from my home province, and they knew that my sister and mother were sympathetic with the new government. The meeting's leaders accused me of not adopting the "progressive" ways of thinking as they had. It was all too confusing so I arranged for Mother to return by train to my sister in Nanchang.

One chilly morning in November 1957, long before daybreak, Lansin, my mother and I set off for the train station. A woman political instructor and two young men joined us for surveillance purposes. Under such awkward circumstances, we could express no emotion. All the way to the station, Mother sat in the car with me, holding my hand tightly. This gesture allowed her to communicate everything she wanted to say to me.

Lansin met us at the station and helped her board the train. At the entrance, Mother turned and casually said,

"Take good care of yourself!"

"Mom! I'm all right. You take care, too." Holding back my tears, I tried to sound cheerful. I watched Lansin escort her grandma to her seat. The train began to move, as Lansin returned. Mother looked at us through the window and waved. I could see her faint smile as the train sped away. I longed to be as strong as she.

Lansin hopped on her bicycle to ride back to school.

"Mom, I'm hurrying to my eight o'clock class. Bye!" She spoke nonchalantly as she had done as a child leaving for school. I understood her effort to ease my mind.

The three "guards" escorted me back to school. My room seemed emptier now, and I was more at a loss.

"Oh, Lord, thank you that Mother is released from this awkward situation. And I thank you that she and Lansin are both strong. But Lord, your hand is heavy upon me. I am at my wit's end. You have promised not to break a bruised reed or snuff out a smoldering wick. Have mercy upon me."

Day after day, I was told to write out my confessions. But I had nothing to write. I refused to fabricate stories.

Late at night, I watched the stars through my window. The familiar constellations were such friends to me. Once I spotted a comet. In a few days it would be soaring far, far away in the depths of the universe. How I wished to fly away, too!

I have had many roles in my life as student, mother, teacher and choir director. But in 1957, in the Anti-Rightist Struggle, I was labeled a capitalist rightist. Little did I know then that I would wear this label for over twenty years! They isolated all rightists for introspection. I could not return to the classroom. Eight hours a day I worked in the kitchen. Nobody dared talk to me. A few other rightist teachers joined me in cooking, but we could not discuss anything or even make eye contact. Morning, noon and night, zealots from the staff took turns throwing malicious, distorted accusations at me. Food had no appeal, and my mind held on to sanity by a thread. Classes continued, but who were the teachers? Who turned my students against me? At night, I was forced to stay in my room like a caged animal. The twinkling stars afforded me some comfort. I could not imagine this kind of torment continuing into another year. How I longed for a change!

One morning I heard a knock at the door and opened it. Li Ming, a young teacher on the staff, stood in the doorway. The camaraderie we once enjoyed had disappeared. Without so much as a "hello" or any eye contact, he said, "Get ready to go to court!"

In silence I followed him out of the building, past the anti-rightist posters that hung from every wall, window, door, and even on ropes between trees — sometimes pasted in thick layers. We walked the two miles to the Intermediate People's Court of Kunming. A young man and woman, acting as judge and secretary, pronounced the verdict, reading from a prepared statement:

"You are convicted of working as a news reporter for

the National Government, of colluding with imperialist elements as a spy wrapped in the cloak of religion and as a member of the counter-revolutionary secret society—the Little Flock Church. You are also accused of plotting to organize the counter-revolutionary teachers' meeting in order to wrest power from the Communist Party in the school. Because you have refused to properly confess your wrongdoings, you are sentenced to be re-educated through labor."

"Oh, my God!" I cried silently. "I don't mind laboring, but for how long? When will freedom come?" The young woman asked if I had anything to say or wished to appeal to a higher court. Clearly, there could be no appeal nor any way to make things straight. Since my God had allowed this to befall me, I would remain silent and leave room for His purposes. Simply shaking my head, I followed Li Ming out of the court. Back at the school, I unlocked the door to my room.

"Pack simple luggage. No books are allowed! Be prepared to leave tomorrow!" Li Ming ordered.

A faculty meeting that afternoon interrupted my packing. The dean announced that all rightists, a few other teachers and myself, were now deprived of public employment. This announcement stunned me. The very status I had worked for and finally achieved in 1957 had vanished like soap bubbles. It had all been in vain!

The next morning, March 8, 1958, I awoke early, rolled up the bedding, and closed my suitcase. All my books, including my Bible, as well as textbooks, reference books and other items would remain behind in a duffel bag, awaiting my daughter's arrival to fetch them. Li Ming walked into my room at about nine o'clock and haughtily glanced at my luggage.

"Are you ready?'

I nodded and said, "Please notify my daughter to come for my bag."

"Let's go!" he said awkwardly; then he motioned to a man to carry my luggage. No doubt this man had been wandering the streets carrying his shoulder pole and rope, waiting for someone to hire him for just such a task. In the old society he had been a coolie, but in the new society such labels and classes were eliminated.

I walked out of the room, down the stairs and across the sports field to the gate. My eyes swept around the compound for the last time. This place, once so familiar to me, had become foreign. I bade farewell in my heart to the school where I had worked hard to achieve public recognition as an official teacher.

"Good-bye, teaching career," I said to myself. "Now I face an unknown future looking up to God my Savior. He will never forsake me."

We took a bus eastward to the outskirts of Kunming, to Dabanqiao, and walked from there. It was early spring on the southwest plateau of China. The warm sun, soft wind and green hills soothed my heavy heart. Eventually, we turned off the highway onto a dusty road. Never conversing, Li Ming deliberately kept a distance of several feet from me. He occasionally asked directions of other travelers. As I trudged along, my mind busily reviewed the events of the last eight months. It had been necessary to send my old mother back to my sister in Jiangxi. She left me with a sad burden in her heart. I blinked back tears. Then I thought of Lansin, whom I had not seen for months. How would she endure the backbiting from her classmates when they heard about me? Would her innocent heart be able to stand all the twisted accusations? I hoped she would find the comforting note I had hidden in my Bible.

As evening came, some houses appeared on the horizon, silhouetted against the fiery glow of the beautiful sunset. My weary steps, cheered by this view, pushed forward to my next destination. It was dusk when we arrived at the farm. Li Ming entered the farm office to complete the transaction, and then left, without so much as a "good-bye."

In the farm kitchen, the cook ladled up a bowl of cold rice and cooked vegetables. The oil lamp provided little light so I could not see what I was eating. The long journey left me starved. I dug into the food with my chopsticks, only to discover that the green vegetable was mostly cooked garlic leaves, something I had never tasted before. The pungent smell nauseated me. I carefully sorted out the cabbage leaves to eat with the rice.

After eating, I was led to a large, roughly built room. About sixty women, young and old, all wearing ragged clothes, crowded into narrow spaces between the double-shelved beds. Under the shadows of a flickering oil lamp, they washed, smoked, talked, quarreled and cursed. A line of people took turns using a urine barrel in the corner. The strong mix of odors from sweat, smoke, stale air, soap and garlic-smelling urine hit my nostrils with a blast. Pausing a moment at the door, my heart sank. Everything was so unfamiliar and unimaginable. I just couldn't accept my situation. Turning my gaze upward to the dark blue vault of heaven, vast and clear, I saw all my precious acquaintances winking down at me. There was the Great Bear, and over there, the Hunter. The Lion and the Queen were twinkling as always, and there was the Scorpion, the most beautiful of all. I addressed them one by one in silence.

"Thank you, thank you! Since childhood, you have been my faithful friends. I am not alone." My God drew near me through His wonderful creation. Quickly walking to my new bed, a bottom bunk made of four pieces of six inch wide boards, I unpacked my bedding, folded my quilt into a narrow sleeping bag, and crawled in wondering how I would ever get to sleep!

The oil lamp extinguished itself, for the night was far

spent. I found the stench and snoring unbearable. Yes, I had longed for a change, but not this. My future appeared as black as the night. Only the stars in my memory, so bright and shiny, restored my sense of gratitude. I thanked God for the night and for the bed to rest. Then my favorite hymn, which Mona and I sang when I left Dali, came to mind:

All the way my Savior leads me,
What have I to ask beside?
Can I doubt His tender mercy,
Who through life has been my guide?
Heavenly peace, divinest comfort,
Here by faith in Him to dwell.
For I know what e'er befall me,
Jesus doeth all things well.

Oh! Merciful Lord, the burden is heavy and I am weak. I need your help!

苦幹爲生

7
Labor to Live

When you pass through the waters, I will be with you; And through the rivers, they shall not overflow you. When you walk through the fire, you shall not be burned, Nor shall the flame scorch you.　　　　　　　　　Isaiah 43:2

Shouldering a hoe at high noon, the sweat dropping down to earth, who would ever stop to think, by looking at the meal on the plate, that every grain is from labor?
　　　　　　　　　Chinese poem

The shrill blowing of a whistle pierced the quiet of early dawn.

"Report to work! Report to work!" shouted someone outside. These sounds, reminiscent of a military boot camp, abruptly woke me. My eyes opened and tried to adjust to the darkened room. Heavy blankets or mattresses covered the paneless windows, keeping out the cold as well as the light. The sounds of people dressing, rushing out the door, grabbing hoes and setting off for the fields prompted me to follow suit. I hurried out of "bed," quickly dressing, and followed them outdoors into the halflight of dawn. Only a few large, heavy hoes remained leaning under the eaves.

"Line up! Get your hoe!" Taking hold of a hoe, I could not help comparing its bulkiness to the lightweight, handy hoes others held. This one was not suited to my frame or strength. My first thought was:

"I am not off to a good start in this new place! I must keep alert and be aware of everything happening around me."

A crowd of workers had gathered. As I approached them, I noticed all eyes fixed disapprovingly on a strong, elderly woman whose clothes betrayed her former station in life as a coolie. She stood smiling triumphantly with a small, shiny hoe raised high in the air. To me, it seemed she was pleased to have been among the first ones to report that morning and would have an easy time laboring with such a fine hoe. Just then a young prostitute piped up,

"So that's why I could not find the small hoe this morning! You must have hidden it!" she accused.

This little scene gave me a preview of life in the labor camp. In Chinese traditional society, Confucius had affirmed loyalty, forgiveness and goodness. Jesus taught the Golden Rule when it came to the way people should treat one another. The social order had now been turned upside down. The new privileged class included the uneducated, the criminal, the soldier and the worker. Even thieves and prostitutes enjoyed a higher status than I did as a teacher. Without restraint imposed by society or religion, backbiting and quarreling became the order of the day.

"Today, break soil lumps. Break them into small, egg-size clumps," yelled the team leader. His poor grammar and broken Chinese revealed his lack of education. He was middle-aged and spoke firmly to us, "You will have 10-minute breaks in the morning and afternoon. Group leaders, take care of that! Now, go to work!"

Following the group leaders into the nearby fields, we began the assigned task. My heavy hoe found the yellow, clay-like soil resistant to its blows. Several vigorous hits were required to break just one lump into small pieces. By mid-morning, my arm muscles, unaccustomed to such work, ached persistently. My blistered palms begged for some relief. I wrapped them in my handkerchief and painfully continued the task at hand. When the team leaders called us to break for lunch and we headed back to camp, water was uppermost in my mind.

"Whoever wants water for washing, follow me! I have saved some in my basin," an elderly woman announced loudly but pleasantly. Several women joined me in taking her up on the offer. She had a large basin full of clean water with yellow mud settled on the bottom.

"I saved this water last night when they brought water. Come on! Bring your basins!" The women gathered around her, eagerly holding out their basins and talking at once:

"I want some! Give me some!"

I stood watching, with my basin in hand, pondering this place and its scarcity of water.

"Wait! Wait a minute! This woman is a newcomer. Let her have some!" She nodded in my direction. I gratefully held out my basin so she could pour me a little. The remaining was shared among the other eight women. Everyone received enough to wet a towel. This woman's thoughtful generosity stood in sharp contrast to the selfishness of the strong woman, who could readily have managed my cumbersome hoe, yet selfishly grabbed the lightest and best hoe for herself and paraded it for the rest of us to envy.

Later, I learned that the kind woman who shared her water had been the maid and cook for a wealthy family. Her attitude was unselfish, and she recognized that I was a decent person. I never forgot the bit of water she shared with me that first day.

Lunch consisted of some rice, rationed vegetables and clear soup. Since politeness and good manners no longer existed, it came as no surprise to see that the first-comers had scooped up most of the cabbage leaves in the soup. Only a few remained floating on top. We were allowed to eat as much soup as we wanted. I had worked up quite an appetite so I relished even this simple food. Laboring in this camp might prove beneficial to me.

Lord, I will be able to do all things set in front of me through your strength.

In time it became clear that a contented spirit, despite circumstances, was key to survival. Those who could not accept the loathsome situation became hateful. They allowed themselves to be "eaten" from the inside out. Their health declined and many died.

I wrote my daughter immediately:

Dear Lansin,

I arrived here at Dabanqiao Farm on the evening of March 8 and started preparing the soil for potato planting the next morning. There are hundreds of people here to be re-educated. One fifth of them are women. In addition to thieves, prostitutes and other criminals, there are rightists from schools, factories, hospitals, etc. Everyone is busy laboring in hopes that it will speed the re-education process. We are free to talk as we work, but the labor is intensive. I'll adjust soon, so don't worry. If you get a chance, try to come and see me. Sunday is wash day and we are allowed visitors on that day.

How are you? How is school going? If you need a change, Mrs. Wong will welcome you for a weekend, I am sure.

By the way, I left all my books, including my Bible, in a big sack at the nursing school. You must find time to go there to fetch these things.

Bye for now. I'll write you again.
                                    Mom

In the afternoon, 500 of us gathered in an empty barn for instruction in growing potatoes. Staff leaders taught seed selection, preparation, digging, sowing, manure spreading, field management and insect control. The next morning the entire farm turned out to begin the task of planting 200 acres in potatoes. In Chinese the first "battle" of spring sowing is called "high tide." We say, "The whole year's work depends on a good start in spring." Long, demanding hours in the field meant I slept well at night and my mind was at ease.

The rush of planting potatoes was followed by the "battles" of sweet corn, peanuts, rapeseed and soybeans. Then a more urgent task of transplanting rice seedlings came. The farm needed to reclaim dry land into paddies in order to enlarge rice crops. The strong men soaked and prepared the new paddy field. Once it was readied, we women were to wade out into the paddies and plant rice seedlings. Most of us were city dwellers, and so this kind of life was completely foreign to us. Many women hesitated to step into the water. There we stood, reluctant, on the edge of the paddy. I recalled some familiar lines of poetry referring to rice planting and thought how interesting it would be to experience it in reality. After all, the farmers did it, and so would I. My Lord Jesus would help me. I removed my shoes and socks, rolled up my trousers and stepped determinedly into the paddy field. My feet were submerged in the mud, and the cold water nearly reached my knees. I shivered. The other women gradually stepped in and we started the planting. Old rice paddies were soft like bean curd, but this newly reclaimed paddy was hard on the feet and made the planting process difficult. Sometimes we had to scratch a small hole in the soil with a finger in order to insert one bunch of seedlings so they stood tall and straight in the water.

From dawn to dusk we bent our aching backs planting seedlings. Eventually, our swollen fingers sprouted thick and wild fingernails. Because of the manure and human excrement in the water, one of my thumbs became badly infected. I bound it in my handkerchief, tolerated the pain and continued planting.

In order to fulfill the production quota, we worked extra hours and even missed washing day. This meant there was no free time. Since I had written Lansin to come and see me on wash day, I worried that she might come when we were in the fields. Then there would be no possibility of our meeting and she would have wasted a trip.

We all made our greatest effort to fulfill the task, leaving us utterly exhausted. No one dared lower his guard and be accused of slowing the spring planting. The least laziness or negligence could be attributed to one's political attitude and might result in being labeled a counterrevolutionary.

My joy and gratitude knew no bounds when Lansin and her boyfriend Liwei visited me. Having finished the rice planting project, we once again had Sunday as our wash day. Liwei's willingness to accompany Lansin to the labor camp touched me deeply. I thought he must be a young man with insight and good judgment, because my bad political situation could have caused trouble for him and his friendship with my daughter. Most people avoided contact with relatives here, and quite a few people had been divorced by their spouses.

Lansin and Liwei brought me things I needed: vaseline, soap, gloves, towels and vitamin pills. We could not talk freely, and time was short. Lansin told me of her plans to go on a geological survey soon. Liwei gave me his address and told me to write him if I needed help. I bade them farewell and they left.

Thank God, it was such good timing! Two weeks earlier or later, this precious visit would have been impossible.

One morning a few days later, we were preparing to go to work. The team leader came to call names. I listened carefully. Yes, there it was,

"Duan!"

As my mind pondered the meaning of this, he yelled, "Those people on the list must prepare to set out for another camp!"

This unexpected announcement caused quite a stir in the camp. A busy hum arose as everyone speculated on the whereabouts of our destination.

"Eat first, and quickly! You'll be going on foot!"

A long march meant I could not take all my belongings. Since it was summer, I decided to take one blanket, a sheet, and some summer clothes wrapped in a big sheet of oilcloth that could be easily carried on my back. I tossed a few odds and ends in a bag clutched in my hand. The remaining things I left behind in a suitcase with my name on it. This bag I entrusted to an elderly woman, Dayang, a former primary schoolmaster whose name had not been called. She promised to care for it as long as she could. Of course, nobody could tell what would happen next!

After breakfast, we set off in columns of two. There were about two hundred people accompanied by soldiers with rifles. We walked westward, skirting Kunming. The soldiers knew that most of the prisoners were from this area, and they could easily lose control if the route went through the city. By late afternoon, I recognized the old familiar road past Lansin's boarding school and on to Chejiabi where the Bible school once had been located. Sure enough, just at sunset, we marched through the village. At this point, I could hardly put one foot in front of the other. My mind and heart, dulled by the circumstances, could not grasp the irony of it all. Here I was being marched at gunpoint past the very place that had been most like home. Only the vague sense of a good memory sounded somewhere deep in my soul. After eight years, the same Mount West, with its features like Sleeping Beauty draping her hair in the lake, stood stark and unchanged against the radiant sunset. I lagged far behind the rest, and was one of the last to arrive after dark.

The final destination was Mount West stone quarry, just behind Sleeping Beauty. We were herded into an abandoned building with more than a dozen rooms. Even with broken doors and windows and damaged walls, it was in better condition than buildings on the labor farm. We organized ourselves in sleeping spaces 20 inches wide on the bare concrete floor. Like a swarm of bees, everyone rushed to get the best places. I stood back a little until they settled, then took what was left. After a simple supper, I hastened to unroll my oilcloth between two other women. Then I spread the sheet on it, putting half of my blanket underneath me and the other half on top. I slept well.

Early the next morning, we awakened to the sounds of explosions and whistles. We understood that it meant time to work. We all hurried out to be assigned to our groups. The worksite, a huge barren mountain slope, must have been dynamited and worked over multiple times. The place was rocky and sandy, with very few trees and sparse stubbles of grass clumped between stones. The high cliff was hollowed out, and leftover crushed bits of stone and sand were beaten into a solid transporting road. The slope was a 30-degree angle, 200 yards long and 15 yards wide. The bottom extended to a large worksite near Dian lake. Rocks of all sizes were piled separately, ready to be shipped by trucks or steamers to construction sites. As I surveyed the lake, I remembered the times as a free person when I had come here on sightseeing trips. A virtual fairyland existed below the surface of the clear blue water.

On a higher cliff, men cut holes to install detonators and dynamite. Planned explosions could be heard in the evening or before dawn. Then the laborers spent the day clearing up the site, sorting the rocks by size, and loading them on the trucks.

This morning's explosion had deposited different-sized stones and sand, all mixed together. Each laborer received two dustpan-shaped baskets and a shoulder pole. Two pieces of rope tied the baskets to the pole. Some laborers transported the huge stones and the sand. Our group collected rocks four inches in diameter and carried them with shoulder-poles and baskets to trucks below. Strong men carried huge stones to a place where others chiseled them into appropriate shapes. Older people hammered stones into tiny bits. For everyone, the heavy labor and sharp stones resulted in frequent injuries. My work gloves quickly wore out. Without protection, my fingertips all went skinless. To this day, they have not fully recovered.

One morning the authorities assigned our group of women to transport rocks the size of dog heads down the hill. Carrying a capacity of 10 cubic feet of rocks weighing 800-1,000 pounds, four people pulled backward on ropes attached to the cart in order to slow the momentum. Even so, the cart could easily crush the pilot if it rolled out of control down the steep slope. Knowing this prospect existed, everyone was ill at ease, even the team leader. Finally, she appointed three women to load the cart and two others to unload. The remaining five of us were assigned to master the cart. It surprised me when she appointed me as the first pilot. I had no experience and my 100-pound frame was not as vigorous as the younger group members. The lady who gave me some water in the labor farm was the only one older than I. But I had learned to hold my peace and look up to my Lord.

The Lord is my strength and my shield. I will rely on you, O God. I felt steady inside and turned to the other four:

"We can do it! Let's try our best!"

The team leader looked at me doubtfully. Once the cart was loaded, I put the pulling belt on my shoulder. The other four women held their ropes pensively with brows knitted, waiting for the signal to begin.

"Hold on and pull hard! Don't let go of the cart!" I instructed them.

The team leader repeated my words and added, "Don't violate our standards of safety!"

Knowing she would blame us if anything went wrong, I pulled down on the handlebars tightly with my two hands. In the process, my fingertips cracked and bled. I prayed silently as I slowly turned the cart downward. We were off and running with the first load.

"Out of the way! Look out! Cart coming! Cart coming!" shouted the four women holding the ropes.

The cart gained speed on the steep slope, and we were losing control. Suddenly, I heard a man shout:

"Go diagonally! Go diagonally!'

I turned immediately and slanted left, then made a 90-degree turn to the right. Two or three turns like this and we gradually slowed the cart at the bottom and halted it right on the spot where others gathered to unload it. How I thanked the Lord for his help. In thinking through the man's advice, I recalled having learned this principle in physics. I consulted with the four rope-holders and told them our plan to lead the cart in a zigzag pattern. The second trip down was much easier. Everyone was pleased with our success. After my third trip, the group leader encouraged others to try. Finally, she tried it herself. After her first trip as pilot, she saw the political cadre coming toward us. She rushed to pilot the cart again. After completing her second trip down the slope, he picked up his loudspeaker and shouted to everyone in the site:

"Attention! Attention! This group leader has demonstrated a very fine way of piloting the handcarts down the steep slope. I congratulate her and encourage the rest of you to emulate her ingenious methods!"

This public praise would look good on her record and would prove her willingness to be reformed. It might even have sped her release.

That evening, during the political study meeting, everyone affirmed the group leader. To my surprise, she expressed her true thoughts about that morning.

"I knew the pilot might be killed. I decided to let Duan Zhi-dao go first. It would not matter much if she were killed since she is a political offender."

She spoke the truth. If I had been killed, they would have said it was because I resisted re-education. Then nobody would be responsible for my death. Deep in my heart, I thought,

"Hard work won't hurt me much. I am safe in the hands of my Lord. You may be unfair to me. You may mock me. The Lord will hold me up and will not make me do something beyond my ability or experience."

The team leader's confession was an example of how people were unashamed to completely expose their cruel thoughts. The labor camp provided a rare opportunity to see what evil lurked in people's hearts. At the same time, I became acutely aware of my own selfish tendencies. But for the grace of God, I could be as bad as anyone. It served as a reminder that a humble heart served one best for enduring the physical and psychological burdens. Two years in the labor camp had taken a toll. I frequently coughed up blood, and like the other women, had stopped having menstrual periods. I could overcome these physical hardships, but having always been outstanding at school as a student and as a teacher, it was especially difficult for me to accept being despised. As a laborer, I was unskilled and had nothing of which to be proud. There was little time for such moments of reflection after working 14-hour days and attending emotional political meetings in the evenings. Hymns I had learned in the past soothed me to sleep each night:

Be still my soul, Thy Lord is on thy side.
Bear patiently the cross of grief or pain.
Leave to thy God to order and provide.
In every change, He faithful will remain.
Be still my soul, Thy best, thy heavenly friend,
Thru' thorny ways, leads to a joyful end.

試 煉

8
Trials

True gold does not fear the test of fire.

Old Chinese Saying

But He knows the way that I take; When He has tested me, I shall come forth as gold.

Job 23:10

One winter morning in 1960, I was told to leave the stone quarry. Five other women also joined me, including the generous woman who gave me water. A truck transported us to a clothing factory in Anning, a small county west of Kunming. About 40 people worked there. Some cut out patterns while others sewed by hand or machine. Relieved to be transferred, I could finally labor at something I enjoyed and for which I was qualified. I had sewn garments for Liuyin and other friends for years, so tailoring would not be as difficult as farming and carrying stones. The living conditions were better and Lansin could visit me more conveniently here. I felt encouraged until the team leader gave me a hand-sewing project. Much to my annoyance, I discovered that my hands were too rough to handle the silk fabric, nor could I hold the needle steady enough to thread it!

A few days later, they tested our proficiency on sewing machines. Twelve of us were chosen to form an assembly line working on the machines while the others cut out patterns, made buttonholes, sewed buttons on, ironed and examined the completed garment. The first product was a man's shirt. A new shirt was to be finished on the assembly line every three minutes. Making the sleeve vents was my assignment. First, I folded the small strips of cut fabric and then sewed the vents on the sleeves. I managed to accomplish the job a bit ahead of every three-minutes. I felt at ease.

The group leader here proved no better than the one in the stone quarry. As a member of the Communist Pary before becoming a rightist, she knew exactly how to be politically correct and gain favor from authorities. She pushed us to work hard while she kept the easier job of examining garments for herself. If she found fault with one of our tasks, she would make life difficult for us. In fact, she worked at torturing us by making the quotas nearly unattainable. Eventually, we made all kinds of clothes for men and women. My assignments became more and more difficult. If I failed to accomplish them in time, the next person in line would be blamed for my delay. The work required all my concentration, and we were not allowed rest. Unavoidably, some sewing mistakes required my working after hours. The strain from working on the assembly line doubled with the overtime. Often my hands kept moving, and my mind remained active in my dreams during the few hours of sleep at night.

There was no way to win. If I failed to accomplish the production quota, they accused me of rejecting reformation. However, if I succeeded, then they gave me harder tasks the next time. I once was required to produce the entire lining for a jacket with an inner pocket in ten minutes. I worked to make a hundred linings per day for several days running so that the quota could be reached. In the end, this tailoring job was no easier than farm work or carrying stones. Here, the ideological pressure to change my thinking proved sharper and more incisive than doing physical labor.

One day, during a visit by Lansin, the team leader picked up the loudspeaker at lunchtime and proceeded to broadcast twisted stories about me. There, in front of my daughter, she accused me of being a saboteur who refused to labor and resisted reformation. While this episode pierced my heart and hurt Lansin, this woman proudly showed the deceit which lurked within her.

That winter witnessed the beginning of the movement called "Great Leap Forward." Young Pioneers attempted to destroy all evidence of the old society. The teachings of Confucius were rejected, and all Chinese were to work extremely hard to increase industrial and agricultural production. The requirements for those of us in the labor camps were even more strict, both for quantity and quality. Now we worked eighteen-hour days for months. On two occasions we worked seven days and nights with short breaks to eat but none to sleep or wash. Many workers had mishaps. I sometimes caught myself dozing while the machine kept running. I thanked the Lord heartily for keeping me safe during this dangerous period.

Working under such strict, unsanitary conditions, I was not surprised when lice showed up in my clothing. They crawled here and there, biting me mostly on the neck and waist. How I longed to scratch to ease this irritation! But I could do nothing while my hands kept busy sewing. Even after working until midnight, what could I do in the small bedroom cramped with a dozen people, sharing only a dim oil lamp? But I had to do something! One day I picked up a piece of wrapping paper and brought it with me to bed. After crawling into bed and lowering my mosquito net, I quickly removed my underwear and carefully folded them in the wrapping paper. Then I put on clean ones and went to sleep. The next day, during the short lunch break, I opened the paper packet in the sunshine and tried to kill all the lice I could see. Since I had only three pairs of underwear, I had to wear them again and again in turns. Every night I put on the pair I searched at noon and wrapped up the ones to kill the lice next day. Unavoidably, there were some survivors roaming in my outer clothes or hidden in seams. I only had one coat and one cotton padded jacket. I wore them every day for that winter. The process took weeks, but I finally got rid of all the lice and their eggs. This troublesome inconvenience, coupled with the strained sewing tasks and mistreatment, brought despair. Tormented in body and shackled in mind, I was on the verge of giving up, when I drew comfort from a Scripture: *"It's true. Suffering produces perseverance, perseverance builds character, and character yields hope. And hope will not disappoint." Thank you, Lord, for this bit of comfort!*

During 1960 and 1961, I continued working in the clothing factory. It was only part of a larger labor camp where the primary function was brickmaking. More than a thousand men, many of them rightists like myself, labored there, treading the slush with their feet and striking it solid with their hands. After inserting the lump into the mold, they shouldered the unfired bricks, load after load, to fill the huge kiln. This labor exceeded that of the the stone quarry in difficulty. Occasionally, we were asked to leave the sewing machines and help make bricks. So I learned the procedures for making bricks: digging, carrying, breaking, striking and molding.

We often had large-scale struggle meetings. Sometimes, certain prisoners were shot to death or sentenced to long imprisonment. Every time, the head person warned us all to make a complete confession of our crimes, or else a similar fate would befall us. An old Chinese saying describes the circumstance: "To kill the chicken in order to frighten the monkey."

I continually felt uneasy and wondered what percentage of all offenses announced was based on fact. Would I be sentenced by all the twisted accusations they made against me? Was I going to spend all my good years in prison?

One evening, too exhausted to finish my supper, I went

to lie down. Just as I reached my room, someone shouted outside:

"Get ready to have a meeting!"

How exasperating! The lack of structure or schedule frustrated me. Anything could happen at any moment. There was nothing to do but forego a nap and report to the meeting. As I was walking with the others to the courtyard outside our workshop, I heard my name. That was strange. Why would my name be called? It was already dark, but a generator kept the electric lights going. I could see several hundred brickmen sitting in close lines around the square, quiet and serious. It appeared that a well-planned struggle meeting was going to occur. Feeling nervous and uneasy, I tried to figure out what it could possibly be. The head person took his seat behind a table, joined by a few activists recruited to mobilize the accusations. Before I could calm myself, I heard my name called in a stern voice by one of them.

"Step forward! Come and stand in the center!"

I pulled myself up, stood straight, and walked to the middle of the circle. My heart tightened and missed beats. In that moment, words from Romans came to mind: "Like a sheep led to the slaughter." Then my ears were assaulted by the loud accusations and slogans shouted by the man and echoed by the crowd.

"Down with the stubborn rightist!"

"Down with the counter-revolutionary!"

"Refusal to confess leads only to death!"

"Don't try to get by under false pretense! Don't pretend to be dead!"

"Make a clean breast of your crime!"

Waves of dizziness swept over me. The scene in front of me blurred and the shouts grew faint until I could hear and see no more. I fell to the ground unconscious.

I woke up on the clinic examining table. How or when I got there, I did not know. I immediately tried to stand

and return to the meeting. Someone stopped me. It was
then that I became aware of two activists in the room
with me. One was the doctor's assistant. The doctor, also
a rightist like me, was standing nearby. He removed the
blood pressure cuff attached to my arm and suggested I
return to my dormitory. Had they sent me back to the
struggle meeting, I could have been more severely pun-
ished for hindering the meeting. As I walked to my
dorm, I noticed that the court-yard was dark. Not a soul
was sitting out there.

Back in the dorm, I found the others in bed and the oil
lamp extinguished. I could only grope through the narrow passage between beds and the wall to find my bed.
As soon as I lowered the mosquito net and sank my face
into the pillow, I appealed to my Heavenly Father deeply
from my heart.

*Precious loving Father God, I thank you and praise you for
shielding me tonight with your mighty hand. The struggle
meeting was meant for me, only for me. It could have been
fierce and violent. And they dismissed the meeting after I was
sick. Thank you, Lord. Thank you! What happens tomorrow I
commit into your hand.*

Instinctively, the beautiful melody of the hymn "Safe in
the Arms of Jesus" came to my lips. I sang it under my
breath.

Safe in the arms of Jesus. Safe on His gentle breast.
There by His love o'er shaded, Sweetly my soul doth rest.
Hark! Tis a song of heaven, borne in a song to me,
Over the fields of glory, over the jasper sea.
Safe in the arms of Jesus, Safe on His gentle breast.
There by His love o'er shaded, Sweetly my soul doth rest.

Tears ran down my pillow. I covered my head with the
blanket and sobbed. The words of the hymn brought me
peace and eventually soothed me to sleep.

I could not confide in anyone. I had learned that lesson
early. One evening a young woman, a college student

and rightist from Beijing National Minority College, walked with me to the place where we washed our bowls and spoons after supper. Someone told me there was a letter on the bulletin board for me.

"It might be from your daughter." she said. "The letter is quite thick. I did not know where to find you so I did not take it."

"Thank you. Where is it exactly?" I asked.

"It is standing on the boardtray of the bulletin board in the passageway."

I thanked her and rushed there with the college student. The letter was nowhere to be found.

"Where is it?" I asked anxiously. "Could someone else have taken it?"

"What is that in the corner on the ground?" she cried out.

There in the corner, in the waning light of dusk, I spotted something white. Bending down, I picked up a torn envelope. In the twilight I made out my name and the words, "Pictures, Do Not Bend." But nothing was in it. I was so disappointed, annoyed and hurt. Some malicious person must have done this. I did not like the idea of strangers, possibly immoral people, having my daughter's photos. How I longed to know what the letter had said. But I could appeal to no one. Thinking the college student would understand, I said,

"What a maddening thing to happen! I don't even know with whom to be angry!"

She seemed to sympathize at the time. Later, however, in a struggle meeting, she twisted this story to prove her good political consciousness and attitude toward reformation.

"I remember hearing Duan say that she has no way to vent her anger here. It is clear she hates being reformed and is holding fast to her counter-revolutionary stand. Her hatred and anger run deep. She is so stubborn...."

The others joined in and agreed with her. While her ac-
cusation might bring an early release for her, it could pro-
long my years in the camp. Of course, I could not retort
or twist others' stories to accuse them. Never would the
team leaders consider me favorably. This experience
taught me a painful lesson referred to in Proverbs 10:19:
"In the multitude of words sin is not lacking; but he who
refrains his lips is wise."

Eventually the high energy required on the assembly
line left me exhausted, and the struggle meetings depressed and suffocated my mind. I fell sick in bed, running a fever. The doctor, a rightist and former superintendent of a large, famous hospital in Kunming,
diagnosed me as suffering from pericarditis. After listening to my heart, he said,

"You must rest. I'll get medicine from the clinic and
send it to you. I will prescribe two weeks' rest for you,
though you should probably take two months off. Without enough rest you could have chronic heart problems."

Grateful to be released from the strain of the assembly
line, I thanked him and went to rest on my bed. I was
alone in the dark dormitory. My thoughts turned to my
loved ones.

A recent letter from Lansin informed me that she and
Liwei had married the previous year. His parents had
been kind and had accepted her despite my being a political offender. I felt deeply grateful. So, this must have
been the message in the stolen letter! What a loss and disappointment. I could not send them presents or even
greetings. Now they lived with my mother and sister in
Jiangxi Province. Since Lansin was expecting a baby, I
was consoled knowing she would have good care. But I
could not help feeling sorrowful in being unable to perform a mother's duty and share my daughter's feelings,
pains and joys. In her letter, Lansin said she regretted
leaving me behind in Yunnan Province and that she often

slept fitfully or cried out at night during dreams of my being tortured, sick, hungry or cold. She even sent me her woolen trousers. I knew she would need them during her time of confinement after the baby's birth.

I imagined my old mother and my sister worrying about me. The very thought brought tears to my eyes. I longed to tell them that I was fine, but I doubted that they would believe me.

Lansin mentioned that they had kept in contact with my dear friend Liuyin. When would we ever have a sisterly chat again? Then I remembered other friends like Mrs. Chong, Mrs. Luo, Mrs. Bi...and the Bible school students! How I longed to see them! Since I could not write them, I remembered them one by one to my Lord.

What a friend we have in Jesus,
All our sins and griefs to bear.
What a privilege to carry
Everything to God in prayer.

Singing hymns comforted me. Without my precious Bible or hymnbook, I could only recall the words treasured in my memory. This precious food kept my spirit alive. Time in bed proved a blessing as I searched for verses and hymns engraved on my heart. I laid my experiences before my Savior. Yes, I knew my unworthiness. Yet, how dearly He loved me and how worthy He wanted me to be. I did not know when the hardships would end nor if I could stand then. Then a wonderful hymn crossed my mind:

Faith of our fathers living still,
In spite of dungeon, fire and sword.
O how our hearts beat high with joy,
When'er we hear that glorious word.
Faith of our fathers! Holy faith!
We will be true to Thee till death.

Yes, I will be true and never lose hope, my Lord. Your grace is sufficient for me. Though bitterness threatens to overtake me, you make my heart sing. Then another hymn welled up from within my soul:

Fresh as the dew of the morning,
Bringing a sweet rest unheard.
Christ in the gentle anointing whispers His
comforting word.
Stand till the trial is over, Stand till the tempest is gone.
Stand for the glory of Jesus, Stand till the kingdom is won.
Lord of all hope, O how sweet is Thy voice,
Making my heart in Thy presence rejoice.

Like a balm that soothed my weary soul, the melody and lyrics immersed me into the deep peace and joy of Christ's dear presence. Though my heart was comforted, my body was wracked with pain. I just could not lie still and had to keep changing my position. Even hard labor was preferable to lying on my aching back.

Three days dragged by. On the fourth morning I woke up from a sound sleep. Feeling somewhat better, I decided to walk to the kitchen to get some food and fresh air. Outside, people squatted in the sun busily eating and talking. The elderly woman who had given me water on my first day walked over to me with her bowl of rice in one hand and chopsticks in the other. She squatted beside me and started to talk.

"We are to move again. Have you heard?"

"What?" I could hardly believe my ears!

"To Fu-an-Cun," she continued. "Their team leader is here in the office. Most likely, they need extra laborers for the upcoming busy farming season. But it is not known which of us will be going."

Just then our team leader, along with a middle-aged woman, emerged from the office door located near the kitchen. Everyone quieted down and listened attentively as our team leader spoke:

"All the women and men named on this list must prepare to go with Team Leader Hou. You will go on foot but two trailers pulled by tractors will transport your bedding."

They called out my name. I couldn't believe it. Moving again! I was grateful that I would not have to carry my luggage, but how far would I have to walk? Could I manage it with pericarditis and a slight fever? So much for the doctor's prescription of two weeks' rest! I could only look to my Lord for strength. Quickly finishing my food, I hurried back to the dorm and painstakingly gathered up my things. I felt weak and wanted to lie down. I sat on the bed for a moment thinking if I had forgotten anything. Others were already loading their things on the trailers. Struggling to my feet, I dragged my suitcase to the courtyard. Some women helped load my things. Then we all gathered in the courtyard. The team leader called out our names once more and then shouted:

"Time to set off. Keep up with the procession! Don't get out of line! Move quickly! We'll reach the farm by suppertime. Now, get going!"

It was two o'clock. We started off in columns of two, with me bringing up the rear. Eight soldiers with rifles escorted us. An old branch found near the kitchen served as a walking stick. The team leader spotted me and walked towards me. Before she could ask me about my condition, my old friend who had given me water again came to my rescue and explained:

"She's been sick in bed for quite a while and only got up today to eat with us...."

The team leader paused for a moment and then said:

"You walk at the back. You may rest on the way but stay together."

I smiled and nodded to her. I was too exhausted to utter a word. How thankful I was for this old woman who could be a companion at this time. Her sympathy was noticeably genuine. With heavy breathing I plodded along the country paths with the others. We avoided the main

roads, walking through cultivated fields. The high al-
titude made for many ups and downs along the way. I
prayed for God's strengthening and sang in my heart a
Scripture put to a Chinese tune:

They that wait upon the Lord shall renew their strength,
They shall mount up with wings as eagles.
They shall run and not be weary,
They shall walk and not faint.
Thank God! *"They shall walk and not faint."*

I pondered God's truth and His faithfulness. Four
hours later, we arrived at the farm, long after the others.
They had already eaten, washed, and were settled. I felt
thankful simply to have completed the task. After eating,
I rolled out my bedding to lie down. I whispered my
prayer of thankfulness half consciously as I fell asleep.
What would tomorrow bring? I could not tell. There was
no time, let alone energy, to worry. The Lord would be
my "very present help."

文藝組

9
Fine Arts Team

Thy sandals shall be iron and bronze; As your days, so *shall your strength be.*   Deuteronomy 33:25

The Lord will strengthen him on his bed of illness; You will sustain him on his sickbed.   Psalm 41:3

Fu-An-Cun was a beautiful village with the Farm of Light occupying five thousand Chinese acres. (A Chinese acre is about one-sixth of a British acre.) Located on a small plateau, the farm was surrounded by vast hills and a windbreak forest in the distance. Crudely built temporary buildings had been erected to house a thousand laborers. Each building had four rows of rooms forming a rectangle around a courtyard. Wooden bunks lined the walls. Armed soldiers guarded the entrances. The two-story farm headquarters building was well constructed. It sat on one side of the dormitories, with the kitchen on the other. We ate our meals there before and after work each day. Once again there were no tables or stools, so we squatted outside or sat on the ground to eat. From this vantage point one could take in the whole panorama: terraced fields, bright green rice seedling beds, lush orchards, nursery stock, vegetable plots and tea plants. Here and there, like well-placed mirrors amidst the greens and browns, one could see the glistening surfaces of the irrigated rice paddies.

It was early spring of 1962, my fifth year of life in the labor camps. I woke up that first morning in Fu-An-Cun feeling in need of the doctor's prescribed rest. In this new place, however, any attempt on my part to avoid labor

would be misconstrued as an anti-reformation attitude.
It could have serious repercussions. I prayed and gained
faith to face the day. My God would care for me. His
eyes were always upon me. I went to work and said
nothing.

By groups of 15 people, they led us out into the fields.
The team leader noticed my weakened condition and
gave me an easier task, seeing that I could not transplant
fast enough to keep up with the competition. My job was
to take the rice seedlings, tie them in bunches of 100, then
deliver them to those who were transplanting. The banks
along the rice paddies were narrow and slippery. Sometimes I needed to step into the water so that the bundles
would reach the workers. All of this posed a challenge
for my bare feet. I could see that even if I were in good
health, I'd be hard-pressed to keep up with these quick-
handed planters.

Some days later I heard my name called from a distance.

"Duan! The team leader wants to see you."

Handing the seedling bundles to someone else, I
picked up my shoes and started back to the headquarters.

"What is this all about?" I wondered.

Arriving at headquarters, I set my shoes outside the
door and entered the building. I then made my way to
the team office door where I called out, "Reporting in,
sir!" and waited to be allowed entrance. After hearing a
man's voice bellow, "Come in!" I entered the team office.
The team leader sat leisurely behind his desk. I stood a
few steps away from him, mindful of my wet feet on the
floor. With an air of superiority, he began to talk to me:

"I have read your records and see that you are capable
of organizing recreational activities. We have received a
notice from the provincial headquarters to form a group
to entertain the laborers as well as perform for villages
and other groups. You are to be part of this literature and

fine arts group. Yaoleng is in charge."

I nodded as I left, thinking,

"How interesting! Yaoleng! Why, he is a famous playwright, and one of his dramas has been made into a film!"

The cold winter wind blew right through me and the stony ground made it hard going for my bare feet. I returned to the dorm, dried my feet, and put on some socks. Then I went looking for the Literature and Fine Arts Group. They met in the so-called reading room, though not a book, a magazine, or even a newspaper could be seen. Seven men and three young women had already gathered. Two men were middle aged like me and the rest were young. I recognized one of the young women as being the former Beijing Minority College student who had once cunningly accused me during a struggle meeting at the clothing factory. The mere sight of her served as a reminder to watch my words. With no space left on the two narrow benches or the table, I picked up two pieces of brick in the corner, put one on top of the other and then sat down on them.

The group leader was indeed Yaoleng. He introduced himself and the others to me. Then he told them that I had formerly taught in the Kunming Nursing School. Most of them were rightists. Only a few of them had been sent to the labor farm for other kinds of offenses. Four of the men, including Yaoleng, were from the famous Art Ensemble of the Military Region of Yunnan Province. They were all high-level artists. The others had some specialty in art, and most of them could sing, act or play musical instruments.

Yaoleng explained that the goal of our team was to build the morale of the laborers. If the workers felt motivated, they would work better and increase production output. Other duties included planning performances for the cultural recreation of the laborers as well as for the peasants and villagers during festivals and celebrations. Our immediate task was to prepare a program for the whole farm in two weeks. We made plans and divided up the work of writing songs, short plays and poems.

I was asked to write some songs. At last, I could spend my days using my brain again, pulling words out of my mind and letting them fall off the tip of my pen onto paper! And then there was the added treat of being able to sit on a bench while I wrote. It had been four years since I had last sat on a bench or chair! This was the Lord's way of giving me the prescribed rest I needed. At first I felt weak and could not do my best. Gradually, I recovered and completed my task satisfactorily. By the time of the performance, I felt strong spiritually and physically once again.

The Fine Arts Team labored half the day transplanting and half the day praising the outstanding workers in song, recitations, clapper talk or comic dialogue. The most popular style was clapper talk. Sonorous rhymes were accompanied by bamboo clappers. When we praised the fastest planters and best-behaved workers, enthusiasm ran high. Everyone worked harder in hopes of accelerating their reformation and gaining an early release.

Each member of the Fine Arts Team needed to work at times as an author, singer, actor or instrument player. We had access to some Chinese musical instruments like the bamboo flute, juqin (two-stringed bowed instrument), pipa (a plucked string instrument with a fretted fingerboard), and a sanxian (a three-stringed plucked instrument). I could not play any of these instruments, but I picked up an accordion which no one else could play. My experience with organ and piano helped me learn to play it. I also learned to speak the Yunnan dialect so that I could act in the "Huadeng" (a type of opera unique to Yunnan Province). Some of the Huadeng songs had been handed down for hundreds of years. I liked them.

Time flew! When the fall rice harvest arrived, we spent more hours in the field cutting rice and sowing wheat simultaneously. I enjoyed watching the plants grow until harvest time. How well the creation manifested God's faithfulness! It never failed to bring forth fruit from the buried seed.

10
Crushed and Bound

A bruised reed He will not break, And smoking flax He will not quench.　　　　　　　　Isaiah 42:3

Come, and let us return to the Lord; for He has torn, but He will heal us; He has stricken, but He will bind us up..
　　　　　　　　　Hosea 6:1

One afternoon, during the "battle of harvest," team leaders ordered us to transport huge electric wire cables from a truck to the storehouse. Like everyone else, I put my head through the huge ring of coiled wire and lay it on my shoulders to carry it. Upon straightening my back, I discovered the load to be too heavy for my small frame. How I managed to get that first load to the storehouse, I'll never know. As I let the coil drop off my shoulders, I felt released from the heavy pressure on my ribs. I took a deep breath and then turned backward for a second load. Just then I began coughing blood. Another worker spotted the fresh blood on the ground. She and another woman accompanied me back to the dorm. My hands turned cold and clammy. They gave me some cold water and then went to find a doctor. During my wait, I was completely alone. I had time to pray and plead with God that He would have mercy on me and sustain me.

A half-hour later a doctor came and gave me an injection to stop the bleeding. I rested but did not feel like eating. That evening Xiao Wen, Xiao Zhu, and Xiao Zhang came for my meal card so that they could get my supper for me. Since wasting food was strictly prohibited here, I tried to eat some soup and rice. Then I asked them to give the remainder to someone who wanted it. When the doctor returned the following day, the bleeding had stopped. He said that he could only give me one day to rest, so the following day I reported back to duty.

We completed the harvest in early November and looked forward to the winter months of reduced labor, when we only needed to collect manure and manage the fields. What a foolish thought. "Labor reformation" could not be so easy. Always, one must fight to work, compete, win—fight with heaven and earth to make your way through. A new "battle" ensued as the "Anti-Rightist Struggle" got under way. Intense political study occupied our "extra" hours during winter afternoons and evenings.

For the first week, we listened to lectures and studied documents about policies regarding confession of offenses and reformation of thought. Later, the names of eight men and four women were announced as the "main targets." My name was among them. Along with the other three people, I moved to a large empty room. Four "politically good people" slept and labored with us. They watched our reactions and were vigilant to keep us from committing suicide. We made our beds on the bare, cracked concrete floor. Not a word was spoken between any of us.

Then, one by one, the twelve of us went through interrogation in front of large groups. Sometimes as many as 2,000 farm laborers watched or shouted as each one of us stood for hours, day after day, listening to trumped-up charges. A young woman was charged with being a spy. She had attended a secret agent school as a teenager, and managed to tire them with her long, detailed stories. The following day she would deny all she had said the previous day. Every day she had a new set of tales to tell. She had practiced what she learned in the secret agent school, and it paid off. Eventually, they tired of her and let her pass.

Others of us did not fare so well. When my turn came, they called into queston my problematic relationship with the "American spy agency" (missionaries) and the "secret society" (Little Flock Church). They also accused me of plotting to seize the Communist Party leadership at the nursing school. I had no reply for these groundless charges and refused to lead them on a wild goose chase as the young girl had with her long stories. There was no way to straighten them out. They became furious. I found it impossible to ignore their scornful faces as they shouted insults at me.

Every night after the tortures of the struggle meeting, I found it difficult to calm down. As I lay in my bed with my eyes shut, their faces and rebukes still filled my mind. I was thankful that my weakened physical condition forced me to sleep soundly. Though I labored every morning with a guard at my side, I felt some release and a restored sense of well-being when I stood under the blue sky, bathed in the sunshine. Fragrant breezes blew about me and I temporarily forgot the fiery trials. Some sense of well-being was restored.

On one such morning, my "guard" said to me,

"You were shouting in your dreams last night. Several times!"

I was surprised and did not know I had shouted. Since nobody else was near, I responded,

"Oh? What did I shout?"

"Nothing that made any sense."

I was grateful, since activists often gleaned clues from those who talked in their sleep. Serious repercussions could result. Finally, after a week of interrogations, they let me go. They concluded that I was stubborn and their final statements included many warnings and threats. I felt helpless and downcast. God held my times in His hands. To think I had put in five years of labor and now had even less hope of freedom.

The Anti-Rightest Struggle ended in December of 1962. Immediately afterward the Fine Arts Team was asked to prepare a performance for New Year's Day to entertain the nearby villages. Every evening we practiced in a big barn with a couple of oil lamps. My jobs were to accompany the singing on the accordion and to play the role of an old lady in a Huadeng opera. I was also the prompter and cared for all the props. On New Year's Eve, we were having one last practice. At one point, while playing the accordion, I felt tired and chilly. I began to cough blood. All the others stopped practicing, frightened by the red pool at my feet. The atmosphere was tense as someone ran for a doctor. After giving me an injection, the doctor and nurse sent me back to my room. My mind flooded with so many thoughts. Was I going to die? Who could take my place in the performance tomorrow? What would happen next?

The following morning, three women from the Fine Arts Team brought me porridge for breakfast.

"How are you feeling?"

"Have you stopped bleeding?"

"We have good news!"

They all talked at once. I smiled and said,

"I'm doing better. Tell me. What is the good news? Have you found my substitute?"

"No! Nobody could take your place. The performance will be on January 4. The Farm Headquarters ordered the doctor to give you the necessary treatment to insure your being fit for that performance. They are going to give you twenty eggs and more than two pounds of sugar."

How surprising! None of us ever had tasted such luxurious foods in the last five years. In fact, there had been no peanuts for years and no meat for at least two years. We cultivated the vegetable plots of sweet peas, carrots cucumbers for the stomachs of the team leaders and staff.

They brought me some water so that I could wash my face, teeth and hands and then left for a meeting. I appreciated their thoughtfulness.

Later, Doctor Zhu came and gave me an injection of glucose.

"I hope you will do well. My task is to guarantee you are able to join the performance on the fourth. So, rest well."

"Do you think I shall be able to go?" I asked.

"Sure, no problem!"

He left. I detected in his manner and voice that his goal was only to please the authorities. He didn't really care about my health.

On January 4 the Fine Arts Team ate an early supper and then set off for the village where we were to perform. Because I couldn't walk to the village with the other team members, the Transportation Department ordered a horse-cart for me. I bumped along the country path, glad when that uncomfortable ride ended. When we arrived, the curtains were already hung on the threshing ground. We performed as planned, but I lost my voice early in the evening. With performances scheduled in two other villages the next two nights, I wondered what would happen.

The other team members returned to the farm for the night, but Farm Headquarters instructed me to stay with certain peasants in each village. After a good night's sleep, my voice returned somewhat. During the day, I helped my hostess with some house-work. I found it so pleasant just chatting with her and sitting at the table to eat. Such simple joys should never be taken for granted. The horse-cart came for me in the late afternoon and took me to the next village. I made it through the remaining performances, but returned to the farm weary and hoarse. The doctor prescribed three days of rest.

The next major performance came at the Spring Festival. Once again we entertained the laborers and villagers several evenings in a row. Though none of us felt cheerful, we did what all actors must do and pushed back our true feelings. We tried to please the laborers, but they could not be moved. They were too heavy-hearted. Traditionally, this festival is the most significant and happiest holiday for family reunions in China. With this being my sixth Spring Festival in labor camp, I could not help feeling sentimental. We ate pork fat for the festival feast. This meager fare must have reminded everyone of the enjoyable feasts of the past. Many had tears in their eyes. "We long for loved ones the most in fine festivals," says a Chinese poem. Any show of sadness was considered resistance to reformation. But how could one pretend to be cheerful? Everybody retired to bed early that evening. Subdued, we couldn't be joyful nor could we reveal our suffering.

The spring sowing campaign followed the Spring Festival. Over a thousand laborers, men and women, gathered to listen to the mobilization speech given by the head of the farm. Part of our task would be the difficult re-claiming of land for rice paddies. He emphasized that this would be a good opportunity for all of us to respond actively and to labor hard in order to reform our reactionary ideology. The outstanding laborers would receive lenient treatment.

By this time I had learned to do all kinds of farm-work. I threw myself into the effort, still too weak to stand for long hours, and my voice was no better. My weight had dropped from 110 pounds to 90. I had the poorest grade of food supplied. Each person ate according to his or her physical build and production. People starved not for the quantity, but for the quality, of food. One time, a former teacher ate his "first grade" portion as well as someone else's leftover food. He died from overeating. His body was not used to so much. Regardless of the grade of food assigned to us, we were expected to fulfill the highest work quota.

I was thankful, I only labored half a day and then worked with the Fine Arts Team in the afternoon. That time provided needed relief. Just when the planting was half done, an order came that the four military artists were to be transferred to the brick plant. The Fine Arts Team was disbanded and the rest of us returned to full-time laboring in the fields.

When I returned to the farming group, Team Leader Hou came to me and said,

"Now that you have returned to the women's team, I want you to be the general measurer. Start today and make accurate reports every day on how much work everyone completes."

She shouted my new position to the rest of the team and I set off to mark where each person had started working so that I could check up at the end of the day. The measuring and calculating I could manage, but the people's temperaments and attitudes proved challenging. Naturally, everybody wanted a good report. I worked hard to be fair and spent time explaining situations. Most of them seemed satisfied with my sincerity and willingness to do the job. Unavoidably, others became captious and rude when my measurement proved less than they expected. There was no point in my becoming angry or arguing with them. I had to just do my best and keep going.

Throughout the varying seasons of the year, I measured all kinds of farm-work: sowing, reaping, weeding, cultivating, winnowing, threshing, composting, fruit-picking and tree-grafting. Some measurements were taken account of by acreage, others by length, weight, volume or number. Toward sunset each day, walking from field to field, measuring, counting, calculating, and dealing with all kinds of people, I felt grateful to be able to meditate on God's goodness and sing to Him.

Abide with me, fast falls the eventide....

Though I had no voice to sing anymore, I let the melody ring in my mind.

Help of the helpless; O Thou who changest not;
Through cloud and sunshine, O abide with me.

告別農場

11
Farewell to the Farm

And the name of the second called he Ephraim: for God hath caused me to be fruitful in the land of my affliction. Genesis 41:52

You brought us into the net; You laid affliction on our backs. You have caused men ride over our heads; We went through fire and through water, But you brought us out to rich fulfillment. Psalm 66:11-12

For more than one-and-a-half years I worked as a general measurer of the women's team and labored part-time. This situation proved favorable to my full physical recovery. One day toward the end of the autumn harvest of 1964, the general team leader stopped by during routine rounds in the fields to talk to me. With a solemn expression he began,

"We have decided to transfer you to the storehouse. You will have the great responsibility of being its custodian. The storehouse contains tens of thousands of kilograms of rice, corn and other grains as well as peanuts, rapeseed, eggs, fruits, cement and gunpowder. You will live in the storehouse and be responsible for the work. Be careful when you distribute any items, especially the cereals and seeds. Most important of all is the gunpowder. Be very strict and check every receipt for the permission and signature of the Team Headquarters. Keep accurate accounts." With these instructions, he left.

The next day, the original storeman turned the entire storehouse over to me. I checked over the stocks, except the grains and cereals. They were piled to the ceiling and could not be weighed. Later that afternoon, I moved my things to the storehouse. It was a large, rectangular hall. Only one door opened in the middle of the long side facing south. Near that door sat a cupboard with account books, documents, receipts, an abacus, and some stationery piled on it. To my delight, there was also a stool so I could sit and work at the cupboard. A single bed sat in a corner.

As I sat down by the cupboard, glad to be alone, I pondered my situation. How strange that I, being a political offender and "class enemy," should be given such a great responsibility! Perhaps the leaders were now less hostile toward me, which meant I would be released someday. Perhaps they feared losing the precious things in the storehouse and had found me to be trustworthy. Whatever their motives, they had given me the key to the storehouse as my own room.

One day, the general team leader came to tell me where to gather duck eggs in the early mornings.

"You must go early before they are taken by others." he said in a low voice as he left.

I thanked the Lord for giving me favor in the sight of the leaders. In fact, none of them had been rude to me, but neither had they rewarded me. They readily praised prostitutes by name, but since I was a "class enemy," they had nothing but contempt for me. One example was Team Leader Hou. Her husband was the secretary at the farm and she had come to the stone quarry to get me. She often discussed matters with me. Once, early in the morning, she found me in the fields and asked me about a certain problem. We squatted there in the grass and talked. She busily took notes until her fountain pen ran out of ink. I offered to help.

"Here, let me see your pen."

Taking it in hand I opened up the cartridge and held it

against a blade of grass still covered with morning dew. The drops of water entered the pen. The ink, though diluted, again ran through the tip.

"Oh, that's a good idea!"

She admired my resourcefulness and willingness to work, but could never express it publicly. What did it matter? I was learning that the important thing was to please God.

My voice remained the same. I could only give my vocal cords a rest by not talking much. Before eating I used a toothpick to poke cotton into my teeth to avoid infection. There was no hope of seeing a dentist or of getting proper treatment of any kind for medical problems.

One morning I received an order from the general team leader to go with the farm truck to town to purchase ropes and gunny sacks. This was an unexpected chance to go to the hospital in town. When I asked the general team leader if I could have my throat checked, he nodded and said,

"You may, but be sure not to miss the truck when it returns in the afternoon."

"Yes, I will consult with the driver. It shouldn't require much time."

I went with the truck and made the purchases. Then I went to the county hospital. The doctor examined my throat and said:

"There is a small blister on your vocal cords. How long has your throat been hoarse?"

"For over a year," I replied. "Can anything be done?"

"Actually, it does not matter much if the blister doesn't grow bigger. It could be removed surgically if your profession demands it. Are you an actress or teacher?"

I knew I could no longer claim to be a professional teacher. I was merely a laborer under reformation. With great disappointment, I said nothing and left.

On the return trip to the farm, the doctor's words kept

resounding in my mind. I could get no help from the hospital. Why had I thought help only came from that source? Why hadn't I turned the matter over to the Lord? I prayed in my heart and asked God's forgiveness and healing grace. I wanted to lift up my voice in praise to my Lord.

In the autumn of 1964, 40 men and women, mostly non-political offenders such as criminals and prostitutes, were set free to go home. How exciting! The rest of us had renewed hope of release someday.

More assignments came my way: keeping accounts for the team mess, being cashier for paying wages to laborers, dealing with registered mail in addition to keeping the daily reports of the work (number of acres planted, watered, harvested, etc.) I had to go to the post office in town to get postal remit money for the laborers who received from their relatives. Once a month, I went to the bank to draw several tens of thousands of dollars in cash to pay wages to all the laborers. I usually returned on the truck. Occasionally, I had to take a train or walk. Even the train stop was quite a distance from the farm. The two-hour walk took me along the highway and partly on hilly paths. It could be dangerous walking alone with cash in such desolate places, but I enjoyed walking alone. My Heavenly Father had His eyes on me so I was unafraid.

By the spring of 1965, the farm had become more productive. Farm Headquarters demanded accurate and detailed reports of everyday production and appointed me to be the statistician. Because I had so much paperwork to do and because the storehouse building was becoming more unsafe, Team Headquarters moved me to a two-room building below the plateau. People worked in the drafting room every day. I was to live and work in the statistician room all by myself.

The house sat in a solitary place with a gully and some

hills behind it. The closest building was a hundred yards away. Chirping insects and howling monkeys punctuated the nighttime peace and quiet. How I appreciated being alone and nearer to my God. I remembered the words of Joseph, who said, *"God has made me to be fruitful in the land of my affliction."*

After the harvest of 1965, a number of us who had worn the "rightist hat" for years were released from the charges and acquired the label of "professional workers." But in reality, nothing changed except our title. I didn't mind laboring, but how I longed for complete freedom.

One benefit of being a professional worker was that we could leave the farm to visit relatives. For the first time in seven years, I paid a visit to Lansin, Liwei and their daughter. They had returned to Kunming two years before. Lansin had graduated from Kunming college of Technology and awaited her job assignment. When I held my three-year-old granddaughter for the first time, emotion engulfed me. I felt as if I had died and come back to life again.

While in Kunming, I had dental work done and visited my original doctor, who had diagnosed my TB 22 years before in the mission hospital. He now ran his own clinic and was trustworthy. After doing a fluoroscopy of my chest, he said,

"The TB focal lesions on your right upper lung have calcified and the edges are fairly clear. Your coughing blood was due to bronchiectasis."

How amazing! My precious God had worked wonders. Hard labor, little rest, poor food and mental pressure could all have caused deterioration to TB. But God had wonderfully healed me. He had also helped me regain my voice. How I praised Him.

As time went on, more people were released to go home, even some rightists. The rest of us anxiously awaited our own day of freedom. In the meantime, I found out that my jobs were to be assigned to cadres of the state, not to a laborer. It appeared they were looking for someone to replace me. The first woman they sent found the job too overwhelming.

In the spring of 1966, I marked my eighth year on the farm. Once again a large group of laborers, including many rightists, was released. But my name was not on the list. Why? Had I done something wrong? Was it because they could not find a replacement for me? I decided to go to the higher authorities at the Reform Affair Bureau in Kunming. The section chief of the bureau, Chief Chen, had been to our farm to give lectures, and I had talked to him once. I made up my mind to go to see him and get the facts. It might worsen things. I could not tell, but I could not keep silent. I prayed for God's guidance and providence.

The next morning, I found the truck parked and being loaded with farm produce. The driver, Xiao Liu, addressed me:

"Duan! Do you need a ride to town? We are going to Kunming today."

I was overjoyed.

"Yes. I have some important errands to do in Kunming. When will you leave?"

"Be back in fifteen minutes."

I rushed to my room, made the necessary arrangements for my work, then hurried back. We set out for Kunming.

I reached the Reform Affair Bureau around 10 a.m. and hesitated outside on the sidewalk. Getting to see Chen might be more difficult than I had first imagined, since I could not enter the building. If I filled out a form, the receptionist would learn my identity and then things could get complicated. I headed down the street away from the bureau. It was nearly 11a.m by now. Suddenly, I had a brilliant idea! At noon the workers left the building to go to lunch. I could catch Chief Chen then. Slowly, I walked back to the bureau and stopped on the sidewalk opposite the gate. The street was wide and had little traffic. I waited until noon.

People started coming out of the gate. Gradually, the numbers increased until a crowd flowed into the street and dispersed in different directions. I scanned the faces in search of a familiar one. At last I spotted him and immediately walked toward him, reaching him in the middle of the street. I wasted no time and squeezed in my request with my greeting.

"Hello, Chief Chen! I want to know about my release."

He looked at me and recognized who I was.

"Your release has been ratified."

"To where?"

"To Kunming."

"Thank you."

With that, he continued on his way. I felt such relief.

Back at the truck, I found Xiao Liu dozing. I climbed into the truck and asked him when we would head back to the farm. He raised his head, rubbing his eyes with both hands and said,

"I'm waiting for one more person."

"Who is it?"

"Secretary Yu."

This Secretary Yu was new on the farm, but I had known him years before. He was a cadre member of the Ministry of the United Front and had worked in religious circles in the early fifties.

While waiting, I ate some oil bread I had bought on the way. Half an hour later, Yu came. He seemed surprised to see me.

"I've been to the Reform Affair Bureau," I explained.

"Oh, I see. Whom did you see?"

"I saw Section Chief Chen."

"What did he say?"

"I wanted to know about my release."

Deceitful as ever, he chuckled and said, "Oh, yes, I know. The certificate for your release is in the Team Headquarters. I meant to call for you sometime after I got back."

"I am right here. You don't have to look for me. I'll follow you to the office. You can help me go through the formalities."

"Yes, we can do that."

"Thank you."

When we returned to the farm, I followed him to the Team Headquarters office and got my certificate. The mess manager, Cadre Wu, a simple young man, looked surprised and asked, "What about the mess account?"

"I have already balanced the accounts for last month," I told him. "Since this is a new month, no bills have been turned in yet. So I am ready to turn it over to you."

"No, not to me. I don't want that job. Someone from the Farm Headquarters will take the job. But she has never done it before. She may need your help."

"Send her to me right away."

It took three days for me to turn over all my jobs to three people, including the woman from the Farm Headquarters who kept the mess account. I taught her how to keep the book accounts and suggested she get help from the accountant at the Farm Headquarters. Now I knew why they had withheld my release.

The labor farm would carry on without me. Those laborers who had no relatives or homes stayed and continued to work. The labor force would always be reinforced with new prisoners. The thieves, prostitutes and other criminals would come and go. My Shepherd had indeed led me through thorny ways to this joyful end.

Part III
Back Home

邋鄉

Bamboo

Stands upright in the wind storm, unyielding.
Hollow center indicates humility and open to new ideas. Over-
lapping leaves resemble Chinese character for
peace and security.

團 圓

12
Reunited

"For My thoughts are not your thoughts, Nor are your ways My ways," says the Lord. "For as the heavens are higher than the earth, So are my ways higher than your ways, And my thoughts than your thoughts."   Isaiah 55:8-9

On June 6, 1966, I bade farewell to the labor camp. I gathered up my few possessions. They were nearly the same ones I had brought on March 8, 1958. With my suitcase, bedroll, and handbag, I climbed into the truck. Most of my acquaintances had already been released, and the remaining women workers were already out in the field. There was nobody to see me off, but I could not delay even a minute to say good-bye. I simply wanted to get out! Outwardly, I showed no emotion, but deep inside I felt great relief.

With my face turned to the future, I pushed back all my troubles and refused to think about them anymore. I must face forward, not look behind, though the next "page" of my life was completely unknown. Re-entering a changed society would not be easy. Teaching was out of the question. What would I do? Where would I go? With such questions on my mind and deep gratitude in my heart, I set out with the truck driver for Kunming.

Lansin had just started her new job assignment in Nanjing, so I had written my son-in-law, Liwei, about my release. He kindly met me at the West Gate Station of Kunming, where the horsecart stopped. Though I had only seen Liwei a few times, I accepted and appreciated him as my daughter's husband. He gently led me to a small house located on a secluded lane. Just off the small courtyard, a door opened to a tiny room with simple furniture. In his quiet and polite way, he explained:

"Lansin rented this room for you six months ago, before she left for Nanjing. With so many laborers being released, she had high hopes that you would soon occupy this place. Maybe tomorrow I can take you to meet my parents and your granddaughter Xiaoming. She is now four years old!"

Imagine! Now I could finally meet these people who had been so kind to Lansin. And Xiaoming, what would she think of me?

He continued, "You know, Lansin hoped that if you returned from the labor camp, you and Xiaoming would join her in Nanjing. I've decided to take two weeks' leave from my office to escort the two of you by train. We'll leave next week, I've already registered you here in Kunming, but I'll have your place of residence transferred to Nanjing."

"Thank you so much!" To think — After 30 years, I would soon return to the city of my youth. I felt grateful for Liwei's willingness to take care of such matters. His tone of voice showed no hint of contempt. Later, when he took me to his parents' home, I was surprised. They welcomed me and did not despise me. I could not remember when I had last experienced such kind treatment. My granddaughter had grown since I had seen her last. She wasn't shy. She greeted me warmly, and went on her way singing and playing happily.

The following week Liwei, Xiaoming and I boarded the train bound for Shanghai. We spent three days traveling together. There was plenty of time for me to sing rhymes and tell stories to Xiaoming. We were getting to know each other. On the third day, at dusk, I got off at Yingtan Station to catch a branch train to Nanchang where my sister and mother lived. My sister would be 40 years old now. Would I recognize her? She had been a 10-year-old girl the last time I had seen her in 1937! As I looked out the train window, my thoughts sped even faster than the wheels. Recollections of the past and hopes for the future surged through my mind. I could not escape the feelings of sadness or shame. What would my relatives think of their long-lost sister and daughter, now 50 years old, having to begin life all over again?

I arrived at Nanchang Station after dark; my brother-in-law met me.

"It is good to meet you at last. I am sorry your sister is not here. She needs bedrest for her pregnancy. She is so excited about your coming!"

We boarded a bus for the remainder of the trip to their home. When my mother saw me coming through the door, she excitedly called out to my six-year-old niece who was sound asleep in bed.

"Deary, Ning! Wake up! Wake up! Look who is here! Great Aunt has come!"

The quivering twang in her voice betrayed her excitement and deep emotion. As I greeted her, my joy-filled heart prayed:

"Oh, thank you, Lord, for uniting me with my dear ones! They have suffered so much pain for me!"

My family showered me with tender loving care during the few weeks I stayed in Nanchang. Trying to make up for lost time, they simply could not do enough for me. The days flew by, and they begged me to stay.

"You should pick up your teaching career again. I could help you get a position here in Nanchang!" my brother-in-law enthusiastically suggested.

"How I wish I could, but I am no longer confident of teaching," I replied thoughtfully. "In fact, psychologically, I would rather do manual labor than teach. Anything that requires speaking and writing is too risky. I have been through painful experiences. The accusations against me were so violent, unreasonable and unbearable."

"Auntie! I don't want you to go! Please don't go!" implored Ning. She sensed the seriousness of our conversation. I pulled her up onto my lap and said,

"I'm not going yet. You are a good girl. Let me hear you sing." I clapped hands while she sang. We were both comforted.

When it came time for me to leave for Nanjing, my sister took me aside and said,

"Sister, take this money. You had no way to save any on the labor farm. Since we don't know when you will work again, let us help you."

I was touched by her thoughtfulness. She and her husband had sent money to Lansin periodically during my eight years on the labor farm. Now she was extending that generosity toward me. I would be forever indebted to her.

How good it was to be back in Nanjing! To be free and to be reunited with Lansin and Xioming was a dream come true. Not without difficulty, Lansin had managed to rent the kitchen room at the home of a vegetable grower. Once again I had the pleasure of living beside a lake. This one was named Bai-lu-zhou, located right inside the ancient south city wall. Trees lined the banks of the lake, which was surrounded by vegetable plots. Willow and peach trees bent their branches into the water on either side of the dike leading to my residence. Standing in front of my new dwelling place, I scanned the willow-veiled lake. Pleasure boats floated on the blue water and various types of arched bridges could be seen here and there. I actually lived in a small park just 15 minutes away from the busy Fu-zi-miao, the Temple of Confucius. The beauty and serenity of this place were almost too good to be true. The room itself was small, with a mud floor level with the outside, where the vegetables grew. Naturally, the damp environment proved to be a perfect breeding ground for worms and insects. While many people found the centipedes terrifying, they hardly bothered me. After facing years of the real horrors at struggle meetings and in labor camps, I had learned to ignore minor annoyances.

Lansin felt sad about my living here. She longed to be able to build me a proper home, but in truth, this simple place suited me. She purchased an old bed, a small charcoal cooker, and a few kitchen utensils for me. Underneath the old city wall, I found some bricks and carried them home. They formed a sturdy foundation for my suitcase. This arrangement kept my suitcase from mildew and provided a table for me. The vegetable grower's wife lent me a bamboo cot where I set food and kitchen things. She and her husband had four children and barely made enough from vegetable growing to survive. They could not afford electricity or running water, even though they lived in this big, modern city. For light, I used a tiny kerosene lamp, a gift from a missionary friend. I fetched water 500 yards away using two buckets and a shoulder pole, a method I had learned at the stone quarry. The two basins I had used on the labor farm served once again in helping me wash my clothes.

I was a spectacle to people strolling through the park. They stared at me with puzzled eyes, wondering what a person like me, wearing glasses and obviously educated, was doing here carrying water with a shoulder pole! Never mind. I had learned not to worry about what people thought of me. I was happy to be where my God had led me. He had made it possible for me to come to Nanjing almost immediately after my release. My son-in-law wrote us that upon his return to Kunming, the authorities had contacted him. As it turned out, he had obtained my transfer of residence to Nanjing from a substitute official. The principal woman in charge of transfers had been on maternity leave and would never have granted it so soon. She had sent a message to the security police in Nanjing regarding this negligence. One day the local police came and sternly interrogated me. It was clear that my political status remained unfavorable. This experience confirmed the fact that I should not return to teaching. After consulting with my daughter and sister, I decided to try my hand at being a seamstress. They helped me purchase a used sewing machine, and soon my vegetable-grower neighbors were bringing their clothes to me for mending. Sometimes I made dresses for their children. Since they were poor and I was not used to business, I never charged them. They brought fresh vegetables to show their appreciation. But in this socialist society, I knew I must get a job soon so that I would not be a burden to my family.

Sometimes I would walk the same route along the street where I used to attend school as a teenager. The school was called Nanjing First Girl's Middle School. I'd look up at the five-story building and remember my classrooms and teachers. My photo had once hung with many others in hallways honoring outstanding students. After the war, however, all such photos were removed.

One day, not far from the school, something caught my eye in a shop window. A middle-aged woman, with her sewing machine right under an open window, was turning an embroidery frame rapidly and skillfully. The needle moved swiftly and gracefully across the cloth, stitching a lovely pattern. She stopped to change her thread and looked up at me. She had a pleasant face which seemed to invite a chat. I expressed my admiration:

"Beautiful work! You must have been doing it for many years."

"No, I only learned last year. It's not difficult. I like doing this job because I can take care of my house and work at the same time."

She patiently answered the questions I asked as well as those I didn't dare ask. Eager to try my hand at her craft, I purchased an embroidery frame, colored threads, needles and an embroidery plate for the machine. At first, my hands struggled to keep the needle on the right track. When evening came, my little kerosene lamp gave insufficient light, so I could only work in the daytime. After a few days' practice I went to the sub-district office and obtained permission for the embroidering job. My first project was fairly simple — to embroider "Little Friend," three Chinese characters in red, on the front of some baby overalls. Gradually, I was able to do more complex designs.

I also worked for a laundry. As a rule, the inner and outer parts of padded jackets were taken apart for washing. My job was to sew them back together. Between the two jobs, I made just enough money to cover expenses. Still, I had no books to read, let alone a Bible. There was hardly time to read the newspaper posted on the city wall. On weekends, Lansin would visit me and tell me the latest news.

The spring of 1967 painted "my" little park in beautiful shades of green and pastels. Notification came regarding a neighborhood sewing group organized to process military clothing produced in a certain factory. Unemployed housewives who owned a sewing machine and were capable seamstresses were promised long-term employment. The good wages and a reasonable and regular schedule of eight hours a day, six days a week, appealed to me. Some people balked at so many working hours, but compared to labor camp, this schedule was easy. I enjoyed the tailoring and could see where my life in the labor camp had tempered me. The other seamstresses, mostly middle-aged housewives with little education, accepted me; but I was not quite one of them.

Life rolled along smoothly for awhile. As summer ap-

proached, the "Great Cultural Revolution" began. Debate
began in the universities and news agencies, then gradually spread throughout the country. Chairman Mao motivated all the teenage middle school students to become
Red Guards and fight. They enthusiastically denounced
people, beat them, confiscated their houses, burned
books (including Bibles) and destroyed everything they
thought to be traditional, foreign or capitalistic. Their targets included machinery, equipment, factories, hospitals,
schools, churches, temples and the homes of the wealthy.
Daily news broadcasts told of high officials, famous professors and organizational leaders being isolated, detained, criticized or tortured. Some even committed suicide. The entire country was in turmoil. The vitality of
the nation was being sapped.

I was thankful that my quiet life among the poor as a
seamstress in Nanjing protected me. Had I been a teacher
or a resident of Kunming, I most certainly would have
fallen prey. Two more years came and went with no
change in the revolution. Life was chaotic, with schools,
factories, hospitals and government offices paralyzed.
Near the end of 1969, Mao's book of quotes, the *Highest
Demand* , was published and distributed. This referred to
Chairman Mao Zedong's instructions during the Cultural
Revolution. Each person was required to carry *The Red
Precious Book* at all times. In every classroom, office, factory or other gathering place, the meeting started and
ended with the participanta chanting certain quotes in
unison. Even while waiting in line for the bus, we recited
Mao's quotes aloud and ended by saying, "Long live
Chairman Mao!" The little red book had to be carried
properly so as to show proper respect for Chairman Mao.
I remember an elderly lady walking beside me on a
street, pointing out to me that she could see *"The Red Precious Book"* was upside down in the bottom of my string
bag. I heartily thanked her for telling me and quickly re-

arranged things in my bag.

Thousands of youth wearing their red-coated uniforms gathered in Tiananmen Square in Beijing, as well as in meeting halls throughout the country, waving their treasured red books and shouting, "Long live Chairman Mao!" They came in waves — a red sea of young people repeating the same dance steps. Mao mobilized the entire country to go to the mountains and rural areas for the socialist construction.

Millions of active teenage students, now Chairman Mao's Red Guards, responded with immense revolutionary zeal. They left their heartbroken parents and the cities for the farms and for desolate, remote provinces like Xinjiang or Nei Menggu. There, they were to settle down for life, laboring as peasants on the land for the sake of socialist construction. These young enthusiasts played their role in the historic Cultural Revolution, unaware of the future consequences.

Tens of thousands of families in the city were mobilized to labor in barren rural areas. Most of them were politically unfavorable people or those who had tangled with their bosses. In the high tide of this movement, every person and every family was required to respond to the call, however unwillingly. Those ratified by the authorities were held up as people to be honored. Northern Jiangxi Province had been announced as the destination for Nanjing residents. I would undoubtedly be chosen to go. The soil there was salty. It would be hard to grow food and to labor to live in that place. I could not see myself spending the rest of my life there. I prayed earnestly and decided to make my choice within the conditions the policy permitted. My hometown, my father's birthplace, in Jiangxi Province was a fertile place with a pleasant climate. I could apply to be sent there to be near my mother and sister.

Nobody could travel during the Cultural Revolution

without permission. When I finally received approval to travel, along with permission to settle in my hometown, I wasted no time in getting to Nanchang. I arrived to find only my mother and my sister's children. My sister was gone for political study and my brother-in-law had already settled in a rural area. He returned the following day and said he had been ordered to move to yet another rural area. When he heard my situation, he decided it would be best if he took my certificate to our hometown to get the permission. This would save me the trip and I could help Mother care for my niece and nephew. He took my certificate and left the following morning.

Mother and I spent that day talking about my hometown. She told me how lovely it was, with green hills, clear streams, good harvests and pleasant weather. The people would be good to me since she had lived there for a few years. She added that someday she would try to join me there. It seemed as though this was my destination, though I could not imagine God's plan for me.

That very night we were awakened by strong knocks at the gate. I opened it, and in came a dozen militiamen in casual clothes, with guns in hand. They shouted as they entered:

"Check residence! Everybody come and show ID!"

My mother handed them the residence booklet, explaining that her daughter and son-in-law were not home and that I was her eldest daughter from Nanjing. I continued our defense.

"In response to the great call of Chairman Mao and the Party, I have come from Nanjing to settle in my hometown."

"Where is your certificate to prove it? Show us your identity."

"My certificate was taken this morning to my hometown to be processed. I do not have it with me."

Then one of the leaders, a man in his forties, stepped

forward and said,

"We are under orders. Anyone without identity is to come to our office for further inquiry. Come on. Get on the truck. We are carrying out a great political movement!"

He waved his arm toward the outside. I could only follow the soldiers along with a few others from the same courtyard. On the truck, we joined dozens of others. My nightgown and cotton padded overcoat proved inadequate now as I sat in the open truck, speeding in the cold wind. They made two other stops to round up people and then took us to our destination.

The darkness, and my unfamiliarity with Nanchang, meant that I had no idea where we were. About a dozen of us were led to an empty room with a smelly toilet barrel in one corner. Four of us were ordered to get rice straw from another room to spread on the bare cement floor. When we had finished that task, the militiaman left the room, gun in hand, locking the door behind him and turning off the light. The room was pitch dark. Some women lay down on the straw and others remained seated. All of us were deep in thought. Since we were strangers, nobody said anything. Everyone anxiously awaited the morning.

After daybreak, we found that our room was in a basement. There were two small windows near the ceiling. We longed to have someone interrogate us so that we could be released. Nobody came, except to lead us out for two simple meals. On the third morning, I received a bag from Mother containing a small quilt, some underwear, a wash towel, toothbrush and toothpaste, comb, soap and paper. How did she know where I was? This circumstance was one more bitter pill for my mother to swallow. How preposterous! Here I was, arrested and detained, without any legal recourse.

On two occasions we were gathered to listen to someone read the newspaper. I learned that the situation was quite serious. A new movement, emphasizing class struggle, was being carried out all over the country. Once a high-ranking official came to the basement and warned us that any who resisted would be killed. A few mornings later we heard a tremendous ruckus outside in the street. Young children shouted:

"Forty shot today! Forty shot!" It was a parade for the death sentence!

The trumpet, the turmoil, the shouting of slogans went on day after day for almost two weeks. Many people were shot daily. Those of us in detention were restless, with questions and misgivings rising in our minds.

What was this all about? Did all those people deserve the death penalty? This was a dangerous question to ask. If my case came before the authorities, they would have no trouble trumping up a charge against me.

It was terrifying and beyond my comprehension.

Oh God, have mercy on me! I am trapped in the bottom of the deepest pit! There appears to be no way for me to soar up and out of here! My faith is small, but I place myself wholly into your hands.

The other prisoners were even more troubled than I. A young girl who had come to Nanchang to meet her boyfriend was arrested for traveling without a certificate. She was frightened and held on to one of my arms almost constantly. One poor woman was so frail. She sold her blood twice a month in order to get money to feed her family. Another woman turned out to be from my sister's neighborhood and knew my mother. She had been detained because only her husband knew where the residence booklet was, and he was gone when the militiamen stopped to check. Some of the housewives had never experienced a situation like this before and needed to talk to someone. Apparently, I looked reliable. They all sat around me. We chatted in very low voices so the guard would not hear. I listened to their stories and tried to comfort them. The young girl and I sang songs. Sharing the burdens of others seemed to ease my own.

The first one to be released was the young girl. Then the woman from my mother's neighborhood was freed. She could update my mother as to the situation. The days in detention crawled by. They were more intolerable and slow than days laboring in the camp. Here, we either attended meetings where people were tried and beaten, or we sat on the straw with nothing to do. I pulled out the nicest pieces of rice grass and wove them into bookmarks to use someday when I would again have books to read. None of the other women seemed interested in this craft project. We were allowed to wash at a sink once a day. Lice crawled on all of us, but there was no way to fight them since there was such poor sanitation. Because we had no privacy at all, I had to change my underwear beneath my quilt at night. My hair and nails grew longer than they had ever been in the past.

Four months dragged by before I was released in the spring of 1970. My mother had written Lansin about my situation. She handled it with my sub-district office and obtained a certificate from them to prove my legal cause for being in Nanchang. In the meantime, my brother-in-law returned with the permission from my hometown to settle there. When they freed me, it was without a word of apology for the inconvenience they had caused. In Nanjing I went to the local authority to begin procedures for the move. My heart was saddened at the thought of leaving Nanjing, where I grew up and was educated. I told him I had been accepted to settle in my hometown, and apologized for having delayed so long in Nanchang. To my surprise, he said:

"The Up Mountain and Down Countryside Movement is over. We no longer handle those affairs."

I did not know what to say.

"Then...?"

"Go back to the sewing group and work as before."

I thanked him and left. So that was how God had worked. He had tucked me away in detention until the storm clouds of this recent political movement had passed.

The following day I gladly reported back to my sewing group. I was shocked to discover that half of them had been sent to the far northern area of our province. My name had been on the list to go with them. Had I remained in the group at the time, I would have been sent. The Lord's ways and thoughts had proven to be much higher than mine.

甘 心 負 軛

13
Bearing the Yoke

Take My yoke upon you and learn from Me, for I am gentle and lowly in heart, and you will find rest for your souls. For My yoke is easy and My burden is light.

Matthew 11:29,30

I returned to the sewing group and worked eight hours a day, six days a week. In my spare time I went to Lansin's home to help care for my grandchildren. Xiaoming was eight now and attended primary school. My fifteen-month-old grandson, Xiaolin, added delight to my life. After all the years of drifting, I so enjoyed the simple pleasures of living near family.

Memories of my past trials often returned to haunt me. Love and praise for my Redeemer would well up in my heart and I would sing a hymn which had been "just the hymn my heart wanted to sing" over and over during the past 20 years. The song was composed by a Chinese pastor who had published many original Scripture songs; I could only remember the first and last verses I had learned in 1949:

Once I was fishing on the sea,
fighting each day with the tide.
When I heard my Lord calling me,
Cast my boat and nets aside.
I love you so, my Lord, you know.
My Lord, you know, I love you so.

'Tis sad to look back to the past,

Now I rush to the Heavenly Road.
My hand may Thou hold fast,
With my yoke, I'm willing to go!
I love you so, my Lord, you know.
My Lord, you know, I love you so.

China had now entered the era called "Great Leap Forward." The entire country was mobilized to contribute all metal items to support steelmaking and the national socialist construction. Pots, pans, nails, utensils, cupboard handles and other items were contributed by each household to be melted. Large steelmaking furnaces were required to do the job. In the late summer of 1971, the government of Nanjing City announced a movement to make raw bricks to construct these furnaces. Each household was to make a hundred bricks. Since I lived alone, I had to complete the task by myself. Experience from labor camp years came in handy. The superintendent of the neighborhood kept abreast of all of us and knew our comings and goings. He also checked on our brick-making progress and arranged to collect the dry bricks for the kiln. The strenuous task of hurling the lumps of soil over and over took hours each day. In the end my lower back suffered from too much bending. No time from work could be given for pain or sciatica problems, so I continued to work with a sore leg. Occasionally, I would get a massage treatment at the hospital. What might have developed into a chronic problem, never did.

There was an old woman in my neighborhood named Gao. She lived with her daughter and often came to talk with me. We became good friends. She was two years older than I and suffered from chronic diseases. She was too weak to work. My ways of talking reminded her of her brother who had attended a Christian college and become a believer. She talked about never having such an opportunity. I felt she was sincere and I felt God calling

me to lead her to Him. So I did, and she accepted cheerfully. We did it secretly. Once she said,

"We must not let anyone know. I won't even tell my
daughter."

It was true! The current political situation put me at
risk if I persuaded anyone to believe in Jesus. It was forbidden. During the Cultural Revolution, there was no religion. Churches and temples were torn down or occupied for other purposes. Bibles and books were burned
to ash. Pastors and priests were sent to labor. This action
could have serious consequences, but I felt I had no alternative. For the first time since my sentencing to labor
camp, I had opened my mouth to confess Christ. I taught
her to pray and wrote out the Lord's Prayer and some
Bible verses stored in my memory. Ultimately, her faith
helped her live through many difficulties.

In 1972 our sewing group was reorganized. Most of the
members were incorporated into a plastics factory. I was
assigned to work with several skilled tailors in a small
shop on Zhonghua Road, the main street in the south
town of Nanjing. It was the same street where I had
walked to school every day in my teenage years. My second grandson, Xiaoyi, was born that year and Lansin
needed more help. She worked eight hours a day and attended political meetings in the evenings. She rode her
bike home six times a day to nurse the baby. I managed
to help her out because I could complete my job in the
evening and be absent for some time during the day. So I
took the older boy, Xiaolin, to kindergarten in the early
morning and brought him back in the afternoon and
freed the babysitter to go home. I stayed with the children until their parents returned after dark.

Life was favorable enough. I had a job to make a living
and could be with my daughter's family often. Once in a
while, I could pay a visit to my mother and sister's family
in Nanchang and stay with them a couple of weeks.

There were still situations in my daily life, however, that reminded me that I was still despised because I once belonged to the so-called "Five Kinds": landlords, rich peasants, reactionaries, evildoers and rightists. Even as a tailor, I was considered "lowest of the low." I still had to be cautious about what I said and where I went. Living in a neighborhood of "good citizens" was different from living in the labor camp where everyone was in the same situation. People looked at me curiously and cautiously. Very few dared get acquainted with me. They called me by my full name. Even young children refused to be polite and showed no respect. By this time, I could stand being called by any name. My status had changed so many times over the years and I had been called so many different names, my heart remained at peace no matter what people called me. Anyway, what did it matter how people viewed me? God was my judge.

I was content being a seamstress as well. God had confirmed my being a tailor by His providence. Yet, I could not forget that I was a teacher at heart. I had once been a person with so many interests and was free to minister in the kingdom of God. I could see no hope at all of returning to that kind of life. At times I felt depressed and resentful, then I would appeal to God.

Why? My God! Why? Is this going to be forever?...

I need Thee every hour...

All my desires for achievement in the world melted away. Now as I neared sixty years old, my youthful dream of acquiring a university education had long ago turned to soap bubbles. It would be ridiculous even to think of it. I could only willingly take my yoke and focus on the heavenly road. He gave me the contentment and hope to keep going.

For China, the decade of the '70s proved to be one of historical importance. In 1972, Richard Nixon, then the President of the United States, was invited to visit China.

Evening political study meetings were held to prepare us for Nixon's visit. We were told not to be too proud or too meek. We must show Nixon how we are building China. So for the first time in 20 years, our country opened to the Western world. This change gradually had an impact on China at every level.

In 1976, Premier Zhou En-Lai, Chairman Mao Ze-Dong, and General Zhu De died one after the other. The Gang of Four tried unsuccessfully to take over the government. Just at the close of the decade, in 1979, a great change occurred.

That particular spring, my twelfth year as a seamstress, a woman came to see me in the small tailor shop where I worked. Mrs. Chu, wife of the former Kunming Bible School headmaster, had sent me cloth shoes from Shangai. This lady came to deliver them. We exchanged pleasantries, and I expressed gratitude for the gift. Just as she prepared to leave, she whispered some exciting news in my ear:

"Sister Duan! Do you know that the first Sunday service was held last Sunday?"

"Really?! Where?" With eyes wide open, I could not conceal my excitement.

"It's on the North Zhongshan Road. Meet at nine o'clock in the morning."

"Thank the Lord! Let's go together!"

Overjoyed, I could hardly wait for the next Sunday. When it finally came, Sister Ye and I went. The place, originally a church courtyard, now served as a truck transportation office. The service was held in a long narrow room that had once been a series of small rooms, but the partitioning walls had been torn down. Now there were about 30 rows of seats with six chairs in each row filled to capacity. Even the standing room was taken and the crowd overflowed outside. Though I recognized no one, I carried the same joy in my heart and tears in my

eyes as they did. The scattered sheep had been gathered
back in His fold. As the prophet Isaiah described,

So the ransomed of the Lord shall return,
And come to Zion with singing,
With everlasting joy on their heads.
They shall obtain joy and gladness;
And *sorrow and sighing shall flee away.*   (Isaiah 51:11)

After the service, I talked with all four pastors. One
was my age, and the other two were middle-aged. They
had spent the past 20 or more years in prison, or factories. When the government's religion department felt
the need to prove to the world that religious freedom existed in China, they chose certain pastors to come and organize the church. Pastor Xu had been living out his
years working in a tailor shop just like me. Now he
seemed elated to be working openly for the kingdom of
God again. When he heard my background, he asked me
to play the piano for him and help direct the choir. What
a joy it was to return again to God's house and serve in
His holy sanctuary! I wanted to shout "Hallelujah!"

The Chinese say, "Not having been practicing for three
days, thorns are growing in your finger." I had not
touched an organ or piano for twenty years! I was not
good at all; but since no one else could do it, I set out to
practice. I played for the services and choir practice every
Sunday. The "Three-Self Church" included Christians
and pastors from many different denominations. Coming
together in this united church, we all felt that God was
having His way.

One early summer evening in 1980, an elderly woman
official from the local district government office down
the street came into the shop to have some trousers
mended. I happened to be alone and so we chatted a bit.
She inquired,

"You don't look like someone who has always been a
tailor. Have you ever had a different job?"

"I have been a seamstress for twelve years now. Before that, I taught."

"That's what I thought! I could see it in your face. You look much more like a teacher than a tailor. What happened to you?"

I briefly told her about being an instructor in the Kungming Nursing School and my years in a labor camp as a rightist. She sympathized with me and commented that the treatment of rightists in Jiangsu Province had not been as strict as in Kunming. This woman and I became friends.

Another customer, Li, a middle school teacher and former rightist, also guessed me to be a former teacher by observing my countenance and ways. He recommended I try to re-enter the teaching field because of the favorable situation and the great shortage.

I weighed these things over and over in my mind. Should I teach again? Twenty-one years ago I had been driven out of the classroom at the nursing school. Did I dare try again? An old Chinese saying brought an image to my mind:

"The sword in the box is waiting for the right moment to fly."

I could see a sword being kept in a box. Would there ever be a moment to fly? Li encouraged me to interview with his friend, the head of the educational department for Nanjing. I recognized his fear in hiring someone like me. He simply shook his head and said he could not help.

I returned to the tailor shop with a prayer: *Lord, have your way then. Shut the door if it is not your will. Amen!*

A few days later, the woman on the staff at the district office returned to the tailor shop:

"Duan, do you want to teach English in middle school? I've been asked to recruit a teacher for a school with an urgent need. I thought of you."

"I would be happy to try," I responded, remembering the sword in the box.

"Good! I'll send the schoolmaster and dean to interview you."

They came the next day and talked with me. Within a few days they notified me that I had been hired as a guest teacher, not a cadre teacher of the state. So I was right back where I had started from — hired by the school but without the status given government-appointed teachers. This time round, however, I was content to remain a guest teacher.

I stayed in the tailor shop for a few more days in order to finish making some of the clothes in my hand. Then I bade farewell to my fellow tailors. They all responded in great surprise.

"What? We never knew you could teach English. Do you still remember after all these years?"

It was true. I could have forgotten all of it for I had not used a syllable of it in 21 years. I purchased an English-Chinese Dictionary and started teaching in the fall of 1979. In addition to teaching three classes of students, I was also asked to demonstrate teaching techniques for all middle school English teachers. My other assignment was to prepare a simple drama with singing in English for a citywide school competition. The vocabulary was simple, and I chose to base it on friendship between Chinese and American students. In the end, the school was rewarded for the successful results of this performance as well as my teaching demonstrations. Never could I have dreamed of doing such things. The sword in the box had flown, and I could only praise God.

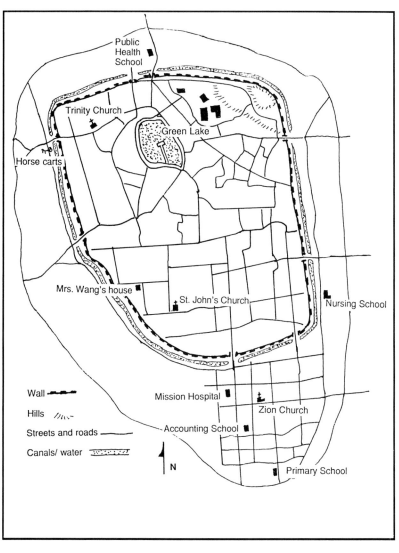

Public
Health
School

Trinity Church

Green Lake

Horse carts

Mrs. Wang's house

St. John's Church

Nursing School

Wall

Hills

Streets and roads

Canals/ water

Mission Hospital

Zion Church

Accounting School

N

Primary School

The City of Kun-ming
(Not to scale)

A

Julia at age 30

Julia's Mother

Julia's Daughter MaoMao and her husband and
granddaughter in 1965

錫安聖堂

Newly built Zion Church
in Kunming

D

Mochou Lu Three Self Church in Nanjing
where Julia was very active from 1979 to 1990

Front entrance to Mochou Lu Church

E

Julia in Spokane, 1993

Julia after graduating from Whitworth College,
Spokane, Washington, May 15, 1994

Psalm 23 in Chinese is in the background.

Frank and Helen Houser visit Julia's daughter and son-in-law in 1994 on their return to China.

G

Julia wears the badge identifying her as a
professor at Nanjing University.

平反

14
Rehabilitation

Behold, happy is the man whom God corrects; Therefore, do not despise the chastening of the Almighty. For He bruises, but He binds up; He wounds, but His hands make whole. Job 5:17,18

Toward the end of 1979, part of a large church building was restored to its proper use as a house of worship. A plastics factory had taken over the church during the Cultural Revolution. To make room for the machinery, the beautiful hardwood floor of the sanctuary had been raised to the balcony level. It was in this upper room, an extension of the original balcony, that we were allowed to meet for worship. Only the very tops of the lovely stained glass windows were visible to us upstairs. By far the larger portions of those windows looked on as the factory workers operated the assembly lines below.

We did not complain, nor could anything dampen our joy. How thrilling it was to gather as believers. We marveled at God's mercy and mighty hand in bringing His scattered children together under His sheltering wing. That Christmas was the first public celebration in twenty years! We celebrated this holy advent season corporately — instead of silently in our hearts as we had done for the past 22 years. We formed a small choir to sing Christmas carols. How good it was to lift my heart and voice to sing the words and melodies I had so loved in my early years as a new believer. It was like rainwater running through a parched riverbed.

Daily, the newspaper published stories of well-known

rightists having their reputations, professions and salaries restored. I dared to contemplate the possibility for myself. After consulting my daughter and son-in-law, I wrote to the Kunming Nursing School to inquire. The answer came in the spring of 1980. A young man and a middle-aged woman visited me. I could not help wondering who they were as I invited them into my simple room and served them tea. Surprisingly, they addressed me as "Teacher Duan." It had been twenty years since I had heard this term of respect attached to my name. They went on to say that they represented the former Kunming Nursing School and had studied my case. They wished to correct matters in person. In a very businesslike manner they assured me that my reputation, professional position, and salary would be restored. Since I was sixty years old now and near retirement age, I preferred staying near my daughter in Nanjing rather than returning to Kunming Nursing School to teach. They agreed and promised to pay me 46.5 ¥ (Yen) retroactively from September 1979. They even expressed regret over my poor living conditions. The nursing school could only help those teachers living in Kunming. I told them that I hoped to move to residential apartments soon.

When these people left, my heart was singing. I had shown no emotion while they spoke with me. But now I praised my Lord for restoring my state cadre status as a teacher. Surely, this was something I had thought impossible. In His time God makes all things beautiful. The Lord gave (he allowed me to get the status in 1957) and the Lord took away (but I never got to teach as a cadre since I was sentenced to the labor farm); blessed be the name of the Lord. He restores the years the locusts have eaten.

Several months later, the nursing school sent me official documents restoring my whole status as an official vocational school teacher, as well as my salary and my reputation. Enclosed was a certificate of retirement and eight hundred yen. With the money, I expressed gratefulness to friends in Kunming who had helped me during hard times. I also bought some books for myself. First I purchased a Bible at church for six Yen. The Liberated Army printed them on the military printing press as a money-making project. I also purchased a few English magazines and a Chinese newspaper. Such luxury. In 1966 the Red Guards had broken into homes and burned all English books. When they began searching in my neighborhood, I burned my English rhetoric book, Longfellow poetry book, and Bible before they reached me. I preferred to do it myself, rather than give them the satisfaction. Now my eyes feasted on the words and pictures. My fingers treasured the mere feel of holding my own books in my hands. At last I would have some use for the book marks I made from rice grass in prison in 1969.

I also bought a short-wave radio. This was the first radio I had ever owned. One evening I turned it on and moved the dial from station to station in search of something that suited my ear. All of a sudden, I heard something like a hymn. I tuned the radio and heard the hymn I had been wanting to find for twenty years: "Lord, you know I love you so..." Overjoyed, I listened to the second, third and fourth verses—the ones I could not recall in prison.

> *Once I was trained by the Lord,*
> *Being led to the mountain high.*
> *I beheld the glorious vision.*
> *I returned not to the world nigh.*
> *I love you so, Oh, Lord you know.*
> *Oh, Lord, you know, I love you so.*
>
> *Once prayed we in the little park*
> *What's there ahead unknown.*

Why watched not me for a little while?
   Let my Lord grieve alone.
I love you so, Oh, Lord you know.
   Oh, Lord, you know I love you so.

Once at the last feast we dined.
   I swore for my Lord I'd die.
But as grave danger confronted,
   Him did I thrice deny?
I love you so, Oh, Lord you know,
   Oh, Lord you know, I love you so.

Joy flooded my heart as I heard this hymn on Liangyou (Good Friend) Broadcasting Station. I listened often to this station.

Stability and effectiveness marked these years of my life. I taught 15 hours each week at a local high school and the technical school. The remainder of my time was spent caring for my grandchildren, sewing clothes for them and ministering in the church. Bible studies and choir practice required time on Saturdays and some week nights. Occasionally, my bronchiectasis returned to warn me not to overwork. These episodes only occurred during vacation times, so I never missed classes.

My sister's daughter was studying at Nanjing University at the time. She stayed with me on weekends. Occasionally, I visited her on campus. My longing for a university education welled up from deep within me as I walked between buildings. The dream could never be achieved at age 60. In my heart I surrendered my desire to the Lord and affirmed my gratitude for His plan in my life. My current life was full and I felt greatly contented.

I could never get over feeling grateful for the opportunity for open fellowship at church. One of my new friends there was Sister Reihua, a professor at Nanjing University. She played the piano beautifully for church services. One day in 1984 she invited me to attend an English Bible study to improve our English. The idea appealed to me. A professor from England hosted the Bible study in the foreign professor's dorm at Nanjing University. The group consisted of expatriate teachers, students, and a few Chinese students. Brother Jeff, an American professor at a pharmaceutical college in Nanjing, proved to be a mature Christian called to serve Christ in China. Eventually, I tutored him in Chinese and learned much from him in the way he served the Lord. He introduced me to Sue, a young American woman attending the teacher training college. Our hearts resonated. She called me "an answer to prayer" because she had been praying for a Chinese Christian friend who could help her. She took me to her college where I met a dozen other American young men and women, all sincere Christians with hearts for God's kingdom. They reminded me of the missionaries I had known in the 1940s who were now old enough to be their grandparents. They were all studying Chinese and could converse, but they knew none of the religious vocabulary and Bible terms. I arranged to help them once a week and so enjoyed this ministry for the Lord.

The summer vacation of 1985 I spent with my mother and sister's family in Nanchang. Ning, now a graduate of Nanjing University and working in Beijing, returned for this family reunion. The joy of being together with my loved ones was dampened knowing that they had no interest in knowing my Redeemer. They tolerated my being a Christian. Only Ning had once mentioned she might become a believer someday. I prayed that the Lord would have mercy on them and that they would turn to Him.

In August I returned to Nanjing only a week before school started. One Sunday after worship, Sister Reihua came over to me and spoke in rather serious tones:

"I have always wanted to help you get a better job because you earn so little. Now there is a chance. The Department of Applied Foreign Language Studies at Nanjing University needs two teachers for the fall semester. They advertised in the newspaper and I have already recommended you."

"No, I am not fit for such a position. You know I am not a college graduate!"

"But you have been teaching for so long. I think you can qualify. The dean of the department wants to interview you this Wednesday. You should at least try!"

Since she had already made the appointment, I had no choice but to go for the interview. I reasoned in my heart that I would never have thought of applying myself. I prayed only that God's will be done.

During the interview, I told the dean that I did not have a college education. He asked me about my teaching methods, ideas and experiences.

Then he said, "According to the university's policy, we need to observe you teaching English for two hours before hiring you. Come on Saturday morning to teach two hours in English at the sophomore level."

I agreed and returned home to prepare the lesson. I could only pray and put forth my best effort. On Saturday morning I arrived at the appointed classroom ten minutes before eight. The dean and two other professors observed the lessons. Since my being hired was nearly out of the realm of possibility, I felt relaxed. I prepared to leave after the lesson. To my surprise, the dean asked me to wait in the adjoining room for a few minutes while they deliberated. He came into the waiting room.

"I am sorry to keep you waiting. We could send you a formal invitation to join the university as a guest teacher. However, that would take several days. The need is urgent, as classes have been in session a full week. Would you mind reporting to work on Monday? We would be most appreciative!"

I consented and promised to do my best. He handed me the freshman English text compiled by Fudan University in Shanghai and helped me with the relevant formalities. I thanked him and took leave. On my way home, my heart was fairly bursting with thanksgiving and praise. How many times had I walked on this campus and coveted the lives of the professors and students? Any possibility to join them had seemed out of the question in this life. All had been too late, too late. A certain Chinese poem expressed my melancholy mood exactly:

"How incomparably beautiful is the sunset.

But alas, the dusk is drawing near."

Now my God had led me to a new task so challenging and unexpected that I rested more confidently than ever in His loving care. A new day had dawned for me. I praised God,

Who does great and unsearchable,
Marvelous things without number.
He gives rain on the earth,
And sends waters on the fields.
He sets on high those who are lowly ,
And those who mourn are lifted to safety.

I went after my new job with a vengeance and thoroughly enjoyed teaching two freshman classes in that fall of 1985. The department never sent me a letter of appointment, let alone a contract. Toward the end of the term, however, I received a time schedule for the next semester. In this way I continued teaching semester after semester.

In 1986 a member of our church choir joined the same department. She had many questions.

"How long are you supposed to teach here? What does your contract say?"

"I don't have a contract nor do I know how long I will teach."

"Why don't you ask for one? A contract provides job security."

"No," I replied. "I am not going to demand one. If God wants me to teach, I can do so without a contract. On the contrary, if God does not want me here, even a contract won't secure the job for me."

In fact, that sister's job lasted only one semester. Year after year, I taught at the university. I learned much from the experience and had a good time with the students. Sometimes they came to my house to chat. All of them knew I professed to be a Christian.

Without missionaries or trained evangelists, the leadership for the growing church looked like Gideon's army. Very few of the original pastors and trained lay workers remained, and we were all around seventy years old. The new seminary graduates since 1989 amounted to only a handful — a mere "drop in the bucket" compared to the numbers of needy new believers who thirsted for more truth. Home Bible studies sprouted everywhere and great crowds gathered every Sunday for worship in the few churches. Obviously, in the rural areas, the homes of Christians became the gathering places for Christians, since no churches existed. Some areas had no preachers at all, and those few evangelists working in these house churches were labeled illegal.

In an effort to bring some control to this situation, the Nanjing Three-Self Patriotic Movement, under the direction of the Religious Affairs Bureau, planned a seven-week training course at our church for new preachers. Fifty candidates were chosen from among those people working in the rural districts surrounding the city. Mochoulu Church was to be the training location, and the entire pastoral team was asked to train them. My task was to teach them hymns. My heart overflowed with simple joy in anticipation of this course. Despite the government's goal to train "politically correct" preachers, I took my task to heart and wanted to do something really helpful for the new preachers. If only I could send them home after the course equipped with a few helpful books, especially the small book called *The Bible Guide*. But nothing of the kind was being published in mainland China at the moment, and how could I get those books from Hong Kong in such a short amount of time? I decided to approach a young American woman, a teacher in the pharmacy college whom I tutored in Chinese every week.

"Christie, can you help me get some books from Hong Kong?" I asked boldly at our next session.

"Yes. Why? What kind of books do you need?" I wrote out a list and told her:

"The most valuable one is The Bible Guide. It is a book written in Chinese by a missionary who knew Chinese very well. Since he could not come to China to preach the Gospel, he wrote this little book. It is written in two parts: the first section gives the concise introduction and outline of each book in the Bible. The second part gives the main theological doctrines with precise definitions and Bible verses. It is simple and clear. I think it will be a great help to the new preachers."

"What do you mean by new preachers?"

"You know believers are multiplying rapidly in the rural areas and there are not enough preachers to lead them. Our church received word from the Religious Affairs Bureau to organize a seven-week training course for those chosen and recommended by the rural Christians. It begins in two days. The Lord put it on my heart to equip them with a few good books. The Life of Jesus is another excellent resource."

"When do you need them?"

"Within seven weeks. After that, they will return to their homes."

"What perfect timing! My friend Pearl in Hong Kong

plans to visit Nanjing some time next month. Let me send your list to her. She may be able to bring the books when she comes. How is that?"

"Wonderful!"

I went over the list carefully and wrote down hopeful numbers and left it with her.

Those seven weeks simply flew by. There was so much crammed into them. Just as the course was drawing to an end, Pearl arrived in Nanjing and brought me more books than I had requested. I was overjoyed to see The Living Water, Streams in the Desert, Fifty-Two Bible Lessons, etc. Then I returned to the church where I got all the candidates names and levels of education. Only a few had high school diplomas. About half of them were middle school graduates and the rest had between 3 and 6 years of primary school education. With this information in hand, I sorted the books and prepared an individualized packet for each one. Each person could have a copy of The Bible Guide and a few other books according to their level of education. I wrapped each of the fifty bundles in brown paper and wondered how to deliver them. This action of mine was illegal and could not be done publicly. The other pastors could not know about it nor could they help. I had to do it alone and very carefully.

The last day of the course arrived. Only the evening graduation service remained, and then they would leave the following morning. I went to the church early in the afternoon seeking for opportunities to deliver the books. I had packed them in two fairly large gunny sacks, and could not bring them in during the daytime while the pastors and other people were around. Finally, I realized that the students would remain alone in the church to eat, while all the pastors returned home for dinner. So about five o'clock I rushed home. Without taking time to eat, I lugged the two bags of books back to the church, arriving at dusk. I was grateful that it was near Christmas time and darkness came early. When I reached the pastors' rooms, I found some of them had finished eating and were already packing in preparation to leave in the morning. I passed out the parcels of books to them. They were all so surprised. Then I had a good chat with many of them and told them they could come to me if they had any problems. I asked them not to mention the books to the other pastors. They nodded their heads and said that they surely understood that. Then we went to the evening service. Thank the Lord! All went well. That evening, I returned home after eleven o'clock and ate my late and tasty supper with great thankfulness. Like a "bird in the hand," God had inspired me and helped me to take advantage of this rare opportunity. Never again has such a training course been held.

From that time on, many of them came to my simple home to have fellowship or to get help. God's love bound us together so that we could serve His church. Imagine! I was a university professor in the city. They were farmers in the countryside. With our very different backgrounds, only Christ could knit us together as co-workers in His vineyards. The intimacy between us could not be kept a secret. A few years later all these rural pastors came to Nanjing to attend a Christian conference. When I entered the dining hall, they all greeted me and wanted me to sit at their tables. The chairman, Pastor Wu, commented:

"They all want Teacher Duan!"

Part IV
Serving The Lord

Chrysanthemum

Blooms in the midst of frost
when other flowers begin to wither.
Hardy, simple and unpretentious,
symbolizes a noble and dignified character.

家庭聚會

15
House Meetings

I beseech you therefore, brethren, by the mercies of God, that you present your bodies a living sacrifice, holy, acceptable to God, which is your reasonable service.

Romans 12:1

My status as guest teacher at the university soon proved advantageous. I had no required Saturday morning classes to teach, which freed me to play the piano for the Shanxilu Church. This church, along with two others, opened in the 1980s. So many new Christians were coming to worship that the main church in Nanjing, Mochoulu Church, could not accommodate them. All four churches started having services on Saturday and Sunday. I had already been playing for the choir practices and Sunday services at Mochoulu Church. The new opportunity to serve on Saturdays at Shanxilu Church meant getting to know many more believers and having opportunities to speak at various meetings there.

After all the years of restraint in the labor camp and tailor shop, I relished these opportunities to serve the Lord. In the Mochoulu Church the services began at 9 a.m. The church held more than 1,000 people, and by 8 a.m., the church was always half full. Rather than waste this time, the church leaders initiated a Sunday school hour during which the people spent the first-half hour learning hymns and the second-half hour hearing Bible stories. They asked me to take charge, and I was happy to do so. Once again the Lord allowed me to combine my musical background with Bible knowledge. By 1992, I

149

had told all the stories from Genesis to II Kings. This teaching opportunity gave me intimate contact with many believers as they consulted me privately about their problems.

Rapid church growth resulted in zealous Christians and new believers starting Bible studies in their homes. Sister Liao, a member of Shanxilu Church, was an enthusiastic new believer but could not read. She invited friends to her house every Monday evening and her pastors came to teach. Such house churches sprang up all over the city. The authorities found it impossible to control such meetings. They declared them illegal and demanded all pastors in Three-Self Patriotic Churches to teach only in their church buildings. In fact, all religious activities were restricted to occur in church buildings.

One early winter morning in 1984, I heard a woman's voice calling me from behind as I crossed the busy Gulou Street. When I reached the wide island, I looked back and saw Sister Liao standing on the sidewalk in front of her shop, desperately waving both hands. It seemed she had something important to tell me. I waited a few moments as she made her way through the rushing traffic to me.

"Thank the Lord. He let me see you! I was busy in the store, when I looked up and saw you in the middle of the street." She let out a long breath. I smiled.

"What is the matter?" I asked her.

"Praise God. You are the very person I prayed for! You know that Pastor Xu announced she cannot teach any longer in my house meeting. And neither of the other pastors is allowed to come to teach. I am having a hard time getting someone to help. I prayed earnestly that God would provide someone. And it's YOU! Please, do come next Monday evening to teach. Please! Please! We all like you, and we appreciate your speaking in our church."

I thought for an instant. What should I say? I already

had my teaching job at Nanjing University as well as duties in both Mochoulu Church and Shanxilu Church. Yet I found it difficult to refuse her and knew I ought not ignore anything that might be of service to the Lord. I prayed in my heart. I must help. "But what will I say to them." I wondered. At that moment II Corinthians 5:15 came to mind:

"And He died for all, that those who live should no longer live for themselves, but for Him who died for them and was raised again."

This Scripture touched my heart at once and I knew the Lord wanted met to share it with the brothers and sisters in this house church. I promised her I would come the following Monday evening. Thanking me profusely, Sister Liao headed back to her shop. I pondered this new commitment and watched her thread her way through the bustling cars, rickshaws and bikes.

The following Monday, at the appointed time, I arrived at her ramshackle home. About two dozen people had gathered. The fellowship that evening proved to be precious. They persuaded me to return the next Monday, and the next. Thus began a journey that lasted for years. We studied several books from the New Testament and grew together in the Spirit. Regardless of the weather, we met for more than three hours. At about 11 p.m. I caught the bus for a 30-minute ride. Then I had a 15-minute walk from the bus stop to my house. Walking alone through the dark streets, my heart often "burned within me," knowing that my life was bound up with the Lord. This work pleased Him. The inconvenience and possible danger seemed minimal since my life was in His hands.

During our study of Romans, one young woman, Sister Pei, said,

"I appreciate very much what you taught tonight about offering our bodies as a living sacrifice. I am so deeply touched. Never before have I heard it explained this way. Oh, how I love it!"

This uncommon response encouraged me. I knew she was a good witness and peacemaker among Christian fellow workers in the factory. She thirsted for the truth, listened attentively and grew steadily. Eventually, she began her own house meeting on Wednesday evenings so that her unbelieving neighbors and Christian friends could hear the Word. Mature Christians helped her, and I equipped her with a few choice books. Eventually, she taught the house church herself.

Another house church had its beginnings at Nanjing University. Every Wednesday Sister Reihua and I met in a quiet spot in the school garden under the shade of a large tree. We shared spiritual experiences, personal problems and church situations. One morning, she told me about Brother Hui and his wife Sister Huai. As the leader of the Christian fellowship at Jinling University, he was the first person arrested, but was detained for only a short while. Since then, he had encountered many trials. He and his wife dared not attend a Three-Self Church though they longed for God's Word and for fellowship. Sister Reihua suggested we meet with them once a week. We met in Sister Reihua's house first. Within a few weeks we grew to fourteen partakers, mostly college professors, all bound with the same love and faith.

The issue of house meetings came up at a Christian conference in Nanjing. At this meeting the Religious Affairs Bureau announced its policy to make house meetings illegal. Everyone needed to acquiesce. However, Sister Liao spoke up and admitted that she had friends in her home to study the Bible. Because she came from a very poor background, the Communists found her trustworthy. She and her husband had started a business. She had eventually become rich and had turned her life over to Christ. Now she had become a hero as she helped street people and opened her home to the needy. She could never fall out of favor with the authorities. After Sister Liao spoke up, I also added some comments:

"Having house meetings can help those who cannot read to learn to read the Bible. They can help people who have troubles to get them solved through brotherly fellowship in Christ. They can help people live in harmony. And that is just what we should do to improve the stability of the society. The government has said that unity is the central task for the whole country."

The simple people and lay leaders in the conference agreed and treated me with warmth. I still sensed, however, that the authorities did not thoroughly trust me. Even so, the house meetings continued and were blessed.

不速业客

16
Strange Visitors

Be strong and of good courage; do not be afraid, nor be dis-mayed, for the Lord your God is with you wherever you go.　　　　Joshua 1:9

During these years God led me into various ministries, and I felt certain I was doing His will. Two hours daily were spent walking and riding the bus to and from Nanjing University. Most evenings found me back on the bus to reach a house meeting. Younger brothers and sisters often marveled that a woman in her late sixties could keep such a schedule. Most of them were married and had access to bicycles for transportation. But I could not forget the years on the labor farm when I worked twelve or more hours a day with no break for weeks. And for what purpose? Now, I was free to serve the Lord. It was surely worthwhile even if I had to work harder. Laboring on the farm had taught me the secret of handling hardships: to be content with all situations.

My living conditions had not changed since 1966. I still lived in the tiny, dilapidated room in the park. The place was dark and dank. If I even so much as dropped a pair of socks on the damp, mud floor, they would be too wet and dirty to wear. The walls and roof were poorly constructed. I could see the sky right through the ceiling and the wind, rain, and small creatures found easy access into my home. For whatever reason, the promised, new residence building had never been constructed. One of my students, a reporter for the Nanjing Broadcasting Station, paid a visit to the headquarters of the park to confront the authorities about my living situation. In China we call journalists kings without crowns because they have power without authority. For this reason, they listened to my reporter friend. Within a short time the park officials moved me into a room in a temporary single-story building.

This new room was 14 meters square, with a makeshift kitchen of 12 meters attached to it. It was not as damp as my previous room, though I could still see the sky through my ceiling and had to walk a block back to the park to use the toilet. This new dwelling place was an improvement over my former home, but it was still inferior to those of my neighbors, colleagues and friends. Despite this fact, many visitors came through its doors for fellowship, Bible studies, and celebrations. Even foreign friends were happy to come once a week for a Chinese lesson and a simple meal with me. Of course, my Christian friends from the rural areas felt very comfortable in this simple home. Setting up a cot in the kitchen, they could stay for the night. We would talk past midnight, sharing with one another and discussing problems they faced. They often brought their friends to meet me and came bearing such gifts as eggs, peanuts, vegetables, chickens and fish. We would cook and eat together. They called me either Sister Duan or Teacher Duan. Once one of my neighbors asked me,

"You teach in Nanjing University so you naturally have foreign students visit you. Why do you also welcome peasants from the rural areas who call you Teacher Duan? How can this be?"

It was difficult to explain. And how could I account for the other foreigners who came? They had learned about me from my friends in Hong Kong and they came to visit me while in Nanjing. Sometimes they delivered bags full of Bibles and other pieces of literature that were so precious to us and so desperately needed by Christians ministering in the vast rural areas.

One autumn afternoon in 1986, an extraordinary thing happened. Two strangers, a young man in his late 20s and a young woman in her early 30s, were brought to my home by the head of our Neighborhood Committee. Her countenance was sober as she introduced them to me.

"These two comrades are from the Public Security Bureau of Nanjing City. They want to see you." I nodded and welcomed them into my home.

I was astounded. Why had they come? I had no time to think and asked them to be seated, one in my rattan chair and the other on the couch. As I poured them some tea, I silently thanked the Lord for teaching me to be calm in critical situations on the labor farm. I remembered the hymn in my heart:

For I know whate'er befall me, Jesus doeth all things well."

As with everyone who visited me, they seemed surprised by my humble living conditions and immediately launched into this topic of conversation. They could see that I had only a bed, a wardrobe, a desk, a bookshelf with a lot of books, and a small pump organ. I had no television, refrigerator or washing machine. Yet, I was quite satisfied and it proved to be a natural way for them to express their concern for me. They sincerely hoped I could better my living situation soon.

Obviously, I could not ask them their purpose in coming. Because they were public security officials, they had no need to explain this to me. The woman appeared to be the senior official and did most of the talking. During our visit, I learned that they knew all the names of my foreign friends as well as every foreigner who came to Nanjing. They also knew that I taught at Nanjing University and was heavily involved in church work. They politely addressed me as "Teacher Duan," and told me they had much to learn from me and wished to be my friends. It was kind of them to say so. When it came to political matters, her casual manner became more serious:

"You know that the imperialist countries have never abandoned their desire to overturn us. We, the patriotic citizens of China, must be alert always to their possible infiltration. If you find anything questionable or have any trouble, let us know and we will help you."

They gave me their hot-line telephone number which I have kept for many years but never used. I thanked them for their generosity and sincerely told them that all my foreign friends were good Christians. I knew they did not value people by religious belief and might think me pedantic. But I knew I would never do anything to harm my country nor would my Christian friends. The only possible charge they could bring against me would be for my religious activities. Since I was following God's will, He would care for me. I need not bother what they thought of me. However, I knew that they had come for surveillance purposes and to warn me. Things could be serious, and other people would consider this a dangerous sign. I decided not to mention it to my daughter or anyone else. They would worry, and it could change the way they related to me. After this episode, the woman who headed our neighborhood committee stopped addressing me as "Auntie." She dared not be as friendly as before, since a visit from these officials must mean I had a serious problem. None of my other neighbors knew, since the officials had not been in uniform.

After this initial visit in 1986, the same two officials returned to my home every few months to check on me. They always dressed in casual clothes. Every Christmas and Spring Festival they brought me presents, a calendar and some nice things to eat. The young man once noted that he chose calendars with pictures of children, cats or scenery since I would not like ones with movie stars. I, in turn, presented them with church calendars which had Bible pictures and verses on them. Eventually, I gave each of them a Bible as well. Their visits grew more natural and friendly with time. Perhaps, as they got to know me, my sincerity convinced them that I posed no danger to the government. Even the woman heading our neighborhood committee returned to her old friendly ways again. I did not blame her for her years of reticence. In all these things I saw the Lord's care for my life.

育 新 苗

17
Young Disciples

For you see your calling, brethren, that not many wise according to the flesh, not many mighty, not many noble, are called. But God has chosen the foolish things of the world to put to shame the wise, and God has chosen the weak things of the world to put to shame the things which are mighty.
I Corinthians 1:26, 27

When Christmas of 1986 came, our Senior Fellowship, comprising college professors, celebrated the Holy Birth of Jesus in my home. Nobody would have dared consider doing such a thing during the Cultural Revolution. So this was the first time to celebrate it at home since the early years after the liberation in the early '50s. Some of the professors' children (college students or graduate students) came along. Each person brought a small present for the gift exchange. I prepared nuts, candy and fruits for refreshments. Once everyone had arrived, we started with worship and sang Christmas carols. Some of the elderly teachers gave testimonies which were so valuable to the young people. We pantomimed stories from the Bible. I presented riddles and questions from the Bible and asked each person to recite a Bible verse containing the word "love" or sing a favorite hymn. Then it was time for the gift exchange. Everyone was excited. The gifts had been numbered, and I had prepared Bible verses to correspond with the numbers. Each person drew a number to receive a gift and a Bible verse. Both young and old joyfully received the special gift and seemed inspired by the Bible verse message.

As everyone was leaving, Brother Chi's son James commented:

"This has been such a meaningful and unforgettable time. I have never had a Christmas like this!"

"Wouldn't it be nice if we could get together like this more often?" chimed in another young person.

"Yes! Yes!" A few others agreed. "We need to know more about the Bible!"

So it was decided that I would meet with the young people every Thursday evening to study the Bible in English. Long ago the Lord had laid on my heart the desire to minister to young people; now He was opening the door. Sister Reihua and Brother Chi came along to help. The young people brought their schoolmates and good friends. Soon we were more than a dozen. Since we could not buy English Bibles, I was thankful for God's provision of NIV New Testaments via visitors from abroad. We started with John's Gospel, then Acts and Romans. We studied one chapter at a time.

Each meeting began with singing songs such as: "For God So Loved the World," "He Shall Feed His Flock Like A Shepherd," "Father, I Adore You," and "Heavenly Father, I Appreciate You." Then we went over the text and everyone repeated what he or she had learned regarding the truth. Then we closed in prayer. As the years passed, we celebrated Easter and Christmas together. We also added songs and hymns to our repertoire: "Amazing Grace," "How Great Thou Art," "I'd Rather Have Jesus" and "I Don't Know About Tomorrow." This last song proved to be everyone's favorite, so we memorized all verses. The chorus held such comfort:

"Many things about tomorrow, I don't seem to understand. But I know who holds the future, and I know He holds my hand."

We could see that these young people were growing in their faith. During these years, few young people attended church. Some of them became believers in their families, but they knew very little of the Bible and hymns. They were happy to worship in homes. Gradually, they started coming to church and helping me minister there. Many of them helped transport books and Bibles brought by friends from abroad. These young disciples were always available to help me handle the heavy bags. Of course, brothers from the rural areas and other provinces often came to take bags to their homes, too. God provided for the safety of His work.

Once some Christian friends from Hong Kong offered me 18 bags of Bibles, commentaries, and other spiritual literature. Since they had to leave the next day, I had to make a quick decision. I decided to accompany them immediately to the train station to deposit all the bags in the "left-luggage" offices temporarily. I kept the tickets so that they could go their way the next day and I could pick up the bags later, after contacting people to help. Many believers came to help, both young and old. We prayed for safety and made careful arrangements. The next evening, three young brothers accompanied me to the train station. We picked up half of the bags and hired a taxi to carry them. Brother Ro and I took the taxi while the other two went back by bike. He sat in front and I sat in the back. We did not get far before being stopped by an armed soldier of the People's Liberation Army who was on duty. I learned later that they were out to catch people carrying contraband goods, especially cigarettes. Two armed PLA men came over and asked Ro,

"What have you got in this taxi?"

"Books."

"What is the destination?"

"Nanjing University."

Then one of them walked around to my side of the taxi. He peeped in at me and asked,

"Are you from Nanjing University?"

"Yes," I answered. He measured me closely with his eyes and spotted my red badge, worn by all employees of the university. He also looked at the bags and paused, considering what to do. Just then, another PLA man, who sounded very young, shouted:

"What's in there? Books? Get out and let us have a look!"

"All right!" I responded at once. Ro hesitated as I prepared to open the bags. My heart was hanging in the air. Just at that moment, one of the PLA men waved his hand to tell the others:

"Let them go! Let them go!"

The other two also waved us on by. The taxi driver revved up the engine and we continued on our way again. We felt such relief and thanksgiving to our mighty God. That night we managed to get the bags delivered to different homes. The next day we returned to the train station for the other half of the bags. This time we went at noon while it was raining. Most people were eating lunch or taking naps. Everything went smoothly.

I knew that the Chinese government prohibited receiving Bibles and books from abroad and passing them on to others. Though I did it often, I did not intend to violate any law of my beloved country. God simply gave me a burning desire to help others to know and accept our Savior Jesus Christ and then to grow in faith. Moreover, I knew these books contained no political teachings. They were purely religious with the power to make better people out of sinners. I did not need to reconsider my actions since I felt I was doing God's will. I occasionally heard of people in other cities being arrested for doing this, but God had given me the task and I must continue. Though my Christian friends expressed concern for me, I placed myself in God's hands. Since my conscience was clear toward my country, I trusted God to protect His work.

Churches in Nanjing, as well as throughout China, gradually became more and more crowded during the decade of the 1980s. Nanjing Jinling Theological College took charge of St. Paul's Church, where they had Sunday services once a week. Both Mochoulu Church and Shanxilu Church had worship services on Saturday and Sunday mornings. I ministered primarily at Mochoulu Church, where I played the organ at Saturday morning worship. Occasionally, I spoke at Shanxilu Church, where I got to know more fellow Christians.

One morning after the service, I was helping a young girl practice a scale on the organ. A woman in her fifties came over to watch and asked to try. She introduced herself as Sister Dai, a worker on a motorboat that served inland water transport on the lower reaches of the Yangtze River. She had great interest in learning to play the organ. She excitedly explained her interest in the organ:

"You know, I bought a small organ in four octaves and have had it on the boat for a few years. Do you think I can ever learn to play hymns on the organ?"

"Of course you can. I learned to play little by little. I shall be very glad to help you."

I encouraged her enthusiastically because her desire was precious. From that time on, if her boat was anchored in Nanjing on a weekend, she came to church and met me afterward for an organ lesson. She had many questions and learned something new to practice every week. I could see that her heart was really set on it. Within two years, she started to play the melody of the hymns on the organ for the church in her hometown.

We became very good friends and she frequently visited my home, not only for advice about organ playing, but also with questions about the Bible. In fact, my door remained open to all the rural evangelists who had been trained at our church, as well as those from neighboring provinces like Anhui, Shandong, Jiangxi, and Zhejiang. I never visited the rural churches, but people from these churches frequently came to my place to obtain books or to discuss questions. I did my best to help them. Though they had little education and Bible training, they were doing wonderful ministry in their villages.

One such person was Sister Yizhen. She was over forty years old when she attended the training session for 50 rural pastors at Mouchulu Church in 1985. With only two years of primary education as a child, she read poorly and could barely write her own name. She had grown up tending pigs and sheep and was little better than a beggar. Yet the twenty members of her village church in Tongjin chose her as their candidate for the training. After the seven weeks she was to return to that church and assume preaching responsibilities. She came to me the night before leaving.

"Teacher Duan, I don't know what to do. I am willing to serve the Lord. But I could not take notes in class or write answers to the exams. Worst of all, I don't remember what I have learned. What can I do?"

"Your willingness is most important. God will help you. Have you got the *Bible Guide* I gave you?"

"Yes, here it is." She handed me the booklet. I proceeded to show her how to use its brief explanation of every book in the Bible and all the main doctrines. I showed her how to look up the Bible verses under subjects like "God's Love" or "God's Righteousness."

"Read the verses and the brief explanation. During the week, let the Holy Spirit speak to your heart. Then on Sunday tell your fellow Christians what you have learned."

We prayed and she left. Each time she returned with new questions, I could see she had been working hard and was growing in faith as well as ability. God rewarded her eagerness and perseverance. During the next two years, her village church outgrew its meeting place twice! Church members numbered over a thousand, primarily women. Finally, the church moved into an old, deserted barn. The brothers in our senior fellowship installed a sound system in the church and our pastor's wife donated an organ. Before long Yizhen came to me and said:

"God has provided us all our needs: a large meeting place, loudspeakers and an organ. Now I pray God will provide an organ player."

I was really touched by her faith, but could see little hope. Not wanting to discourage her, I suggested that she bring me some of the young girls from the church choir. Maybe I could teach one of them to play the organ.

"Oh! That is just what I was hoping you'd say. I don't know how to thank you enough for all the help you have given me."

"God has been blessing you, Yizhen," I responded. "I can see that He is rewarding your efforts and fulfilling your desires. You have grown up so much both spiritually and in Bible knowledge. I praise the Lord for that!"

With tears streaming, she quickly added, "And I thank Him for preparing such a fine teacher as you to help and love!"

In my heart I earnestly prayed: "Lord, bless her heart and her ministry. Thank you for giving me the privilege of assisting this dear sister."

One early spring Saturday morning in 1990, Yizhen brought three young women from her church to my home. We chatted over some tea, and I sensed that all three were fine Christians eager to serve the Lord. After we had them sing hymns together and separately, it was clear that the high school student was not interested in hymns, and one of them could not carry a tune. The logical candidate was a young married woman in her early 30s. She told me she could play the melody of "Jesus Loves Me" with her right hand but had no idea what to do with her left one. Since she lived almost two hours away by train, she could not have weekly lessons. We got right down to business, and I began by teaching her to find the C, F, and G major scales.

Hours later, Sister Yizhen called us from my kitchen, "Lunch is ready. Come and eat!" I looked at my watch. It was already after one o'clock! So absorbed in teaching music, I had completely forgotten about lunch for my visitors. How lovely that Sister Yizhen had prepared the meal without my even knowing. We ate together and enjoyed the fellowship.

As we were eating, I said, "Thank you so much. Honestly, I rarely have ready-made meals. You have saved me a lot of time and work. Thank you!"

"I do not know what to say," she said smiling. "I owe you so much for all you've done for me. I'll never be able to repay you. I wish I could prepare your meals every day to save your time for serving the Lord!"

After lunch, we returned to the organ lesson while Yizhen cleaned up. They left at 4 p.m to catch the train home. I praised the Lord for the eventful day and entertained hope in my heart.

Toward the end of the year, I had a slight attack of my old bronchial trouble. Sister Yizhen and her organist came for a visit one day and caught me resting in bed. Standing right at the foot of my bed, sister excitedly reported the progress of my organ student:

"She has played the organ for several Sunday services now. God has answered my prayer and provided an organist! Isn't that wonderful? What happened to you? Are you ill?"

"I'll be all right. I just need some rest." I tried to sit up but could do little else to make my visitors welcomed.

"You stay in bed," said Yizhen. "I know just what to do."

"Help yourselves to some tea," I called after her.

"While you prepare it, Yizhen, maybe my organ pupil can play hymns for me. I'm anxious to hear how she is doing!"

So while Yizhen fixed tea, the young woman played all the hymns I had assigned her to practice, along with some others. I was amazed. Despite my weariness, I managed to tell her about sharps and a few other rules we hadn't covered during the first lesson. Of course, Sister Yizhen not only prepared tea, but lunch as well. After they left, I felt encouraged and I rested peacefully.

That day sister told me the entire congregation had been praying for a new church building since the barn was so close to the train station. Elderly church members found it difficult to cross the tracks and the train whistles and rumblings disrupted the services. She informed me that she had applied to the Three-Self Patriotic Movement and the Religious Affairs Bureau for permission. The permission to build a new church came in 1993, and God faithfully provided all the church's needs.

Not only did I see God equipping rural evangelists, but He was also raising up servants in the seminary. The Jinling Theological Seminary commenced classes in Nanjing shortly after the church reopened in 1979. Since the seminary was located only a few blocks from our church, seminary students attended church services and participated in various ministries. I enjoyed fellowship with several of them, including Brother Pei from a small town in North Jiangsu Province. He often visited me and attended my English Bible class. Formerly a middle school teacher of English, he had left his good job when he felt God calling him to attend seminary and become an evangelist. In 1988 he graduated from the seminary and was assigned to work in the main church of Huaiyin City of North Jiangsu.

One day the following summer, he came to visit me. I was anxious to hear about his work. To my surprise, he simply sat in my old rattan chair, holding the cup of tea in his hand, shaking his head sadly.

"I have had no peace serving in this church," he began. "Almost from the beginning, there has been no freedom for me to minister in the way in which God seemed to lead me. In my prayers, it is clear God wants me to leave. I have decided to obey His call once again and leave the church in Huaiyin. What a difficult decision this has been! He will have to help me face the obstacles!"

As I listened to him, my heart understood his dilemma.

"What do you plan to do?" I asked him.

"I do not know. I cannot minister elsewhere since I am leaving without the permission of the Religious Affairs Bureau. Other Three-Self Churches cannot hire me, and the illegal house churches are out of the question."

"Perhaps you could return to your old job as a middle school teacher," I suggested.

"No, it is not possible; and anyway, I do not want to continue teaching."

"How will you make a living, then?" I asked.

"I'll return to my parents' farm in the countryside. Both of them are getting up in years. My wife and two children are living with them. They need someone to do the heavy labor of the farm. We can live on the rice, vegetables and livestock we'll grow ourselves. I shall work there and await God's further guidance."

I appreciated his sincerity and sensitivity to the Holy Spirit's leading. It had been no small thing for him to follow the call of God out of teaching and into seminary. Now, to leave a fixed-wage job in a main church seemed incomprehensible. Yet he seemed confident of God's leading. What a contrast to most other seminary graduates who sought high positions in the large city churches.

"You have made the right decision," I responded. "God has a plan for you and will lead you one step at a time. He is faithful and mighty. Trusting in Him is better than trusting in anyone else. He has promised never to forsake you. And His Word says that those who trust in the Lord shall not be ashamed."

"Thank you for your sympathy and support. You are the only one I have told of my decision."

"I understand. Be assured I will not mention it to anyone else."

Six months later, he came again to tell me that he had started a house meeting in his own home, and God had blessed it. His nephew, also a young seminary graduate, had joined him in ministering there. They had found joy and peace in following God's leading. But the seminary had learned about his leaving Huaiyin Church and had called him back to Nanjing to consult with the supervising professor. After lunch, he headed off to the seminary.

When he returned later that evening, he looked disheartened. It seemed that he was the first graduate of that seminary ever to leave a church assignment. The seminary had been highly criticized by the Religious Affairs Bureau and the professor feared that Brother Pei had set a bad precedent for future graduates. Consequently, the seminary was offering him a job on the editing staff of the "Bible Truth Reader," a bi-monthly magazine sent to all churches in China as well as general subscribers. He had promised to pray about it and give them his decision.

"This would be a good job, and the magazine offers a wonderful service to the churches," he said. "I could live right at the seminary. It is a good-paying job and would give me the opportunity to continue to learn. From purely a worldly point of view, it would be more profitable than digging in the infertile soil of North Jiangsu."

After two days of praying, he came to a decision.

"I have no peace about accepting the seminary's offer," he said. "Yet I have no decent reason for refusing it. I shall return home and write the professor a letter explaining that I am waiting for God's further guidance."

In the end he continued being a farmer and serving with his house meetings. He kept in contact with other rural evangelists and was a source of encouragement to them. He and his nephew frequently visited me to discuss Bible teachings and problems. Christian brothers and sisters in Nanjing joined me in donating clothing, equipment, Bibles and other books to their ministry. As a result, the Lord showered his blessings on us as givers and also on them as the recipients. By 1992, his house needed to be enlarged because over 300 people now attended services there. I suggested that he break it into many small house meetings instead. Though it would require more time and effort to pastor, it would be a more effective, safe route to take.

Not all the trainees fared so well. Yage was twenty-four when he came from his home, a suburb of Nanjing, to be trained. He appeared to be clever, capable and diligent, with real potential as a preacher. After his training, the seminary asked him to stay and work for the "Bible Truth Reader." During his years on that job, I spent time teaching and training him in a variety of ministries. He could do almost anything, as evidenced by the stove he built for me. I had hoped that he could eventually set up a printing press to print Christian literature and Bible study reference material. Those dreams never came to fruition, however, because Yage left the faith. Our pastor had called him "one of the best young preachers" so it was heartbreaking to see him squander his talents. Despite this disappointment I thank the Lord for these experiences and opportunities. My faith has been enriched by the associations with various people: the faithful and the failures, believers and non-believers, men and women, young and old, city and rural dwellers. They are too many to mention, but I treasure them all.

青年聚會

18
Youth Meeting

These things says He who is holy, He who is true, "He who has the key of David, He who opens and no one shuts, and shuts and no one opens."   Revelation 3:7

Go therefore and make disciples of all nations, baptizing them in the name of the Father and of the Son and of the Holy Spirit, teaching them to observe all things that I have commanded you; and lo, I am with you always, even to the end of the age.   Matthew 28:19,20

During Christmas of 1988, our church choir performed a Nativity play in three different churches. Thousands of people came to the celebration, which included drama, Christmas carols and the Gospel. At one performance, the main entrance was completely blocked. In fact, crowded conditions that night caused doors to come off hinges and some window panes to be broken. When it came time for the choir processional, it was impossible for the choir members to march down the aisle, as planned, holding lit candles. We had to climb over a table and over people sitting in the aisle. After a great deal of pushing, the singers finally settled in the choir loft, where they straightened their robes and lit their candles. The only empty space was just beyond the altar; otherwise, there was no place even to set a single foot! It was an amazing experience. During the ensuing weeks, many who attended this Christmas production returned to church services. Most of them were young people.

The entire church staff shared excitement over this turn

of events. We talked among ourselves about what should be done for these young visitors. Then one Sunday after the service, during our monthly staff meeting, Pastor Wu announced that we were beginning a youth meeting in our church. A seminary student named Zhen-Zhen and I were to be in charge. She was a mature Christian with eight years of churchwork prior to her seminary studies. I was taken aback, however, by the announcement that I should be entrusted with such responsibility. Since Pastor Wu announced it, he must have received permission from the Religious Affairs Bureau. A good friend of mine, Pastor Qu, immediately said,

"It is good for Sister Duan to be responsible. But have you asked the Religious Affairs Bureau? What do they think of it?"

"No problem. No problem," Pastor Wu responded. Then he abruptly changed the subject.

I understood Pastor Qu's question. She had learned to consider political situations and was quite sure the Religious Affairs Bureau would not approve of my being responsible. But it was unlike Pastor Wu to make a decision on his own. He must have received some sort of permission before announcing it at the meeting. I knew the Lord had opened the door for me to work. Proverbs 21:1 came to mind: "The king's heart is in the hand of the Lord: Like the rivers of water, He turns it wherever He wishes." I thanked the Lord in my heart. Then I made a few requests of the staff:

"This is an exciting development and I count it a privilege to be given this task. I hope that Brother Yong, vice president of church membership, can help Zhen-Zhen and me. We three will work out a plan and then take it to Pastor Wu for his advice and approval. We will need help from those seminary students doing internships here. And lastly, I would like to include the young members of the choir. This opportunity could provide good training for them."

The staff members heartily agreed. What a great wonder of the Almighty! Nothing like this had happened in
China since the churches reopened in 1979. Now many
young people could hear about God's love and re-
deeming grace. I had longed and prayed for just such an
opportunity! I must not give undue attention to the pros
and cons of the situation but minister wholeheartedly as
the Holy Spirit led me. After consulting with Sister Zhen
and Brother Yong, I returned home to pray and plan.

What would be the best way to deliver the true Word
and the Good News? I drafted a schedule: The youth
meeting would convene every Saturday night from 7
p.m. until 9:30. The first half hour would be spent learning hymns and choruses. The music time was to be followed by worship, which would include a main speaker
giving a Gospel message or the teaching of a main doc-
trine. After that, group would break into four groups:

1. Brother Yong would lead a Bible study group for
those seeking to know the Gospel.

2. Sister Zhen-Zhen would lead a discussion group for
new believers, where they could share their testimonies.

3. I would lead a spiritual discipline group for believers.

4. Seminary students would lead a group where new-
comers could ask questions about believing in God. Others could receive counsel on how to solve personal problems involving marriage, family, job and education. This
would no doubt be the largest group needing the most
time.

Sister Zhen-Zhen, Brother Yong and I all agreed to begin with Luke's Gospel and to concentrate on the life of
Christ. We worked out all the themes and speakers. The
pastors approved of our plan. We began the meetings in
the spring of 1988. About 50 young people attended the
first one. Everything was going smoothly. By autumn,

the number reached two hundred college students, young professionals, high school students and primary school teachers. Though the meetings were to end at 9:30 p.m. many of the youth tarried afterwards for an hour or more, to ask us questions. We understood that these young people had nowhere else to go with their problems. How could we refuse them? This meant that I had to wait another 50 minutes for the next bus home. Brother Yong did not like this situation, and offered to take me home on his three-wheeled bike. Due to the great distances involved, this would take him more than an hour and he would often arrive home to his wife after midnight. There seemed to be no easy solution to this problem.

When the seminary students were assigned to a different church the next semester, many of them returned Saturday nights to help. They all seemed to agree when one of them explained:

"We can see that God is blessing this youth meeting. We want to take part in the ministry here. Besides, we are all learning things, too!"

Even old Sister Chen, a woman in her late 80s and the chair of our church membership committee, once commented:

"We can see that the Holy Spirit is working in the hearts of these young people. It is a great blessing from God. So many people come here seeking the truth on Saturday evening instead of watching television programs or having fun elsewhere. This is precious. Praise the Lord!"

By Christmas of 1989, more than thirty young people were ready to be baptized. We gave them a ten-week series in preparation for baptism, covering such topics as the relationship of God, man and sin; the Trinity, the salvation of Christ; the meaning of baptism and Holy Communion; how to pray and read the Bible; and how to witness for Christ. At the end of the course, they were prepared to be examined for baptism by Sister Chen and the other pastors.

Over one hundred people, men and women, old and young, were baptized in our church on Christmas in 1989. Both old Pastor Wu and old Pastor Ding were weary from bending and sprinkling the water on their heads. Only twenty of our young people were among those baptized. The other ten were Communist Youth League members and we were forbidden to baptize them. The church dared not compete with the Communist Party for the youth, so Sister Chen asked them to wait until their league memberships expired. I knew that the age limit for league membership was twenty-eight. Most of these young people were between twenty and twenty-three. They would have to wait several years to be baptized! By that time, the active ones would have become Communist Party members. They were eager to be baptized now. It grieved me to see them refused.

That night I had no peace. Before God, I was responsible for these souls. There must be some way to get them baptized. Perhaps I could consult Brother Yu and Sister Chian on this matter since they had helped teach the baptism classes. We often had the same mind on things. I was willing to baptize them, but felt a brother should do it. I would ask Brother Yu.

The next morning, after teaching a class at the university, I went to the Yus' home. They invited me to eat with them. So, over lunch, I told them about the ten young people not accepted for baptism and poured out my heart to them. They agreed that we could not wait years to baptize them. Brother Yu, a man of few words, said quietly,

"I think we will have to do it, but I have never done this before."

"God will enable us to do new things to glorify Him," I

assured him.

"Sure, we'll manage. It's a great blessing!" chimed in Sister Chian.

We decided to have the baptism, followed by Holy Communion the next Sunday evening. Brother Yu agreed to get ready for the baptism and communion while Sister Chian prepared the bread and wine as well as the bowl of water and cushions. I was to inform the ten youths and have a personal talk with each of them to prepare them for baptism and to help them have the right attitude toward the church and the political policy.

The evening proved to be a blessing to all thirteen of us. Since it could be a sensitive problem, we never talked about it with anyone else afterward.

By this time, around three hundred young people were attending the youth meeting. Friends told me they overheard people in the city talking about coming to our church on Saturday nights. Another church had started youth meetings on Saturday night, offering more of an entertainment format, supposedly to compete with our more structured plan. All of this meant only one thing: our youth meeting had attracted attention, and that might not be good. As the Chinese proverb says: "Don't get too high or be too noticeable." Like the bird's nest in the tree, once it is seen, it is a ready target.

In the spring of 1991, two visitors came from a church in Zhenjiang City to learn how to run youth meetings. Brother Yong and I sincerely told them that we did not know how to start, but we simply sought God's guidance and the help of fellow workers. I felt unsettled just knowing that people in other cities knew about our youth meeting. I prayed for the Lord's protection and for His will to be done.

News soon reached us from the Provincial Christian Delegates Conference held in Shanghai. Apparently, during the meeting, Miss Jiang, an outstanding professor at

Jinling Seminary and the chair of the Provincial Three-Self Patriotic Movement, praised our youth meeting but questioned my being in charge of it. She stated that such an activity should be the responsibility of a trained pastor. I had met this Professor Jiang since I frequently visited the seminary. She had expressed appreciation for our ministry in the youth meeting. I knew that she was quite influential, since she had worked with Yang Shaotang, a famous spiritual leader. She was loyal to the Religious Affairs Bureau and had the trust of the authorities. I was too busy to analyze all the rumors. God knew my heart.

One day Pastor Wu came to my home. This was quite unusual for him. He had only come once before when I was ill. Since we saw each other so often at church, there was ample opportunity for communicating matters there. He must have something very important to tell me.

"Sister Duan, we have been so grateful for your ministry with the choir, Sunday school, and especially the youth meeting," he began. "I am concerned about your age and health. It must be difficult for you to stay out late on weeknights. Why, I am two years younger than you, and I rarely go out evenings. Since you are getting up in years and are not very strong, I wish to lighten your load. I am going to ask a younger person to take charge of the youth meeting. You may remain as an adviser."

In that instant, all the rumors and recent happenings came together! Pastor Wu must have received some pressure from the authorities. God was sovereign.

"Thank you, Pastor Wu, for coming to tell me," I responded. "I will be ready to hand over the responsibility when you find a replacement for me. There should be no need for an adviser."

After he left, I prayed to quiet down my heart. I could not help feeling pain at the thought of leaving this ministry, but I would submit to God's plan. Later I told Sister Rei and Brother Yong.

"I am sorry to hear this," he said. "I am not surprised, however. Sister Chen recently told me that the authorities had approached the church leaders repeatedly about your being allowed to do so much in the church. I know the church staff has been most appreciative of your help. They will be hard-pressed to replace you. The obvious choice would be Sister Zhen-Zhen, but she is in England with her husband. I am too busy to take full responsibility!"

We all agreed that I should finish out the fall term and take a break. God must have some purpose in closing the door to me. I never returned to the youth meeting and I stayed away from the church completely. I continued teaching at the university and ministering in the house meetings, though my heart arrhythmia problem returned. It seemed that God might be preparing to take me elsewhere to minister. Perhaps I would return to Kunming, where many of my old CIM Bible School students were now pastoring churches. A friend had written that there was a great need for ministry in the university there. I asked the Lord to show me the way.

神行奇事

19
God's Wonderful Deed

To everything there is *a season, A time for every purpose under heaven...A time to keep silence, and a time to speak.*   Ecclesiastes 3:1,7

And now, O Lord, what do I wait for?   My hope is in You...I was mute, I did not open my mouth, Because it was You who did it.   Psalm 39:7,9

My abrupt departure from Mochoulu Church in early 1992 after 13 years of ministry seemed awkward. Many brothers and sisters wondered why I was no longer involved. I told them my health prevented me—which was partly true. But I knew that God ordered my steps at every turn. He alone knew when and where I should start and stop.

That spring, both Pastor Wu and Pastor Ding came one Sunday afternoon to persuade me to return to minister in the church. I promised to consider the possibility when my health improved. To show his sincerity, Pastor Wu suggested I take his place in the pulpit the second Sunday of the following month. I agreed to do this, thinking I would make it my farewell message. Not only would this be appropriate, but it would also make it appear that no prohibitions existed. The concerns of the church members would be eased. I preached on John 8:32, "The Truth Will Set Us Free." I also met with the choir, as well as with the young brothers and sisters, urging them to serve the Lord wholeheartedly. Though I enjoyed fellowship in my home with various church members, I never returned to Mochoulu Church; and the pastors never came to see me again.

At this juncture in my life, I longed to set aside everything and study the Bible. A kind of dryness had set into my soul after all the years of ministering at the church as well as in house meetings. I yearned to return to the green pastures and still waters I once experienced at the Bible School in the 1940s. In those years I knew many Christians from other countries. They had had a tremendous influence on me. Now, some forty years later, God led me to work with a new generation of missionaries. These friends helped me contact the Mackenzies in Australia, the Snows in the U. S., and the Joyces in Canada. Two American couples who taught at Nanjing University in 1988 were very special to me. The Frederichses, a young couple, helped teach my English Bible class. The Housers, a retired couple, helped me contact other Chinese Christians and introduced me to some Chinese people interested in knowing Jesus Christ. They frequently corresponded with me after they returned to the U. S.

In July 1992, Helen Houser wrote me, inquiring about my ministry. I wrote her about my situation and casually expressed my longing to study the Bible. Since there was no possibility for such study in China, I asked her about the chances in the U. S. I did not stop to think about my being 73 years old nor the near impossibility of my getting a passport.

To my great surprise, I received a reply on August 1 with an application to Whitworth College. Helen had obtained permission from the international student office for me to study in the religion department. Mrs. Diane Hermanson had already signed the needed form as my sponsor. She agreed to pay my school expenses and to house me for a year. This news was so wonderful that I found it hard to believe! After a long-distance call to

Whitworth, my sponsor sent the other required form, and I was ready to apply for a passport. Two years earlier, I had applied for one to go to Manila for a Christian Conference. I received no answer at all. As the Chinese proverb says: "Just like a stone dropped into the sea." I wondered if this second attempt would again be thwarted.

On August 18, 1992, I filled out the required forms and handed them in to the Foreign Affairs Office of Nanjing Security Bureau. The young official seated behind the counter wore a brand new uniform with shiny buttons and a bright national emblem on the brim of his hat. In an efficient and confident manner, he checked my forms one by one. He frowned briefly as he read the first page of my application.

"Going abroad to study religion?" he asked, surprised.

"Yes," I nodded.

"Why? Aren't you teaching at Nanjing University? Do they approve of your going? You need a certificate from the school to show their approval."

"I am a retired teacher. I continued teaching for almost thirteen years after my retirement in 1979. For seven years I have been teaching at the university to meet their needs. I am not a permanent staff member, only a guest teacher. There is no bond for my leaving as long as I don't drop teaching in the middle of the term."

He hesitated, then said slowly:

"We have never issued student passports to people over thirty-five years old and never to a religion major not sent by a seminary. Besides, you have been very active in churches. We need to know what the Religious Affairs Bureau thinks of this. You'll have to wait."

I knew the Religious Affairs Bureau's attitude towards me. In fact, they rejected my application to Manila. Later, I learned that nobody from mainland China attended that conference. My heart sank and I returned home in despair.

On Sunday, August 23rd, just five days after handing in my passport application to the Security Bureau, I was walking home from my daughter's house at about 9 p.m. All of a sudden, a swiftly speeding bike whirled out of the dark and knocked me down onto the cement. My right hand and hip struck the ground. The young bicycle rider stopped to help me to my feet. My right side hurt badly and my right wrist could not move without sharp pain. Oh, what a horrible misfortune! How could this happen at such a crucial time in my life? I had no time to think. My wrist needed immediate treatment. I said to the young man:

"Please take me to a hospital. I hope there is not a fracture."

He nodded and let me sit on his bike while he pushed it and continued to converse with his friend. After a bumpy and uncomfortable trip, we arrived at the district hospital only to find their radiology room not open on Sunday evening. We had to go to the city hospital about twenty minutes' walk away. The young man parked his bicycle near the hospital gate and led me into the big building. It was quite crowded.

"You wait here, I'll go register you," the young man said.

Before I could respond, he hurried down the hallway and out of sight. Holding my wounded wrist, I tried to follow him. As I turned the corner, I did not see him standing at any of the registration windows. I walked out the main entrance through the dim courtyard to where he had parked his bike. It was gone! He had run away, probably because he did not wish to pay my medical expenses. How could he leave me in such a helpless situation? In pain and feeling exhausted, I prayed:

Merciful Lord, help me to forgive him. Thank you that my hip is not broken and I can still walk. You will hold me up, Father, for you have led me all the way.

Thus began an unforgettable night in search of medical care. After an x-ray and promise of surgery in two hours, I walked to a different hospital, hoping for more immediate care. At that hospital, the orthopedic resident woke from a catnap, only to inform me that his department was under construction and no equipment was available. I finally reached my grandson by phone. He and my daughter rode their bikes a half hour to reach me. They took me back to the city hospital. The surgeon had already left so they put a cast on my wrist. We returned to my daughter's home in the early hours of the morning.

Three days later my wrist was swollen. It appeared my case was serious and could prevent me from doing anything, let alone going to the U. S. In the end, a contact made by my daughter at the City Chinese Traditional Medicine Hospital realigned the wrist, splinted it, and gave me herbal ointment that proved amazingly curative.

While I was recovering, my daughter managed to find time to go to the Foreign Affairs Office to inquire about my passport. She returned greatly disappointed.

"I am afraid there is little hope for you to get a passport. The official, Comrade Li, talked with me. He seems to know you very well: how many foreign friends you have, how popular you are in the religious circles, as well as your past history. He knows even more than I do! Don't you know your name was filed both in the Public Security Bureau and in the Religious Affairs Bureau?

"Yes, I suppose," I answered.

"Why haven't you ever told us?"

"I didn't want you to worry, nor did I believe it to be very serious."

"Comrade Li said he would come to see you tomorrow, since you are injured."

I spent much time meditating. Comrade Li was one of my "strange visitors," who, along with the senior woman official, had first come to visit me in 1986. They continued to visit me every few months, always in plain clothes. He was the one who had avoided giving me calendars with movies stars. I, in turn, had given them Bibles. He knew my sincerity, so I felt some hope. Though I didn't know the outcome, I wanted to cling to my God and obey whatever way He chose for me.

Comrade Li came the next afternoon. How good it was to see him again. He told me that he learned from the Religious Affairs Bureau that I was neither a paid clergy of the church nor a paid worker of the Three-Self Patriotic Movement. So they had nothing to do with my leaving. He went on to say:

"We consider your request to study abroad a legitimate one. Your passport is ready. You can go and get it tomorrow."

What a surprise! I thanked him and praised God in my heart. As he walked out the door, he exhorted me to be careful about speech on public affairs abroad. I must remember that. But I could not imagine the reason they permitted me to go. It was God's wonderful deed!

Two days later, with passport and certificates in hand, my daughter and I boarded an express train for Shanghai. It was necessary to apply for a visa at the American Consulate there. Because it was closed for the American Labor Day, we had time to contact Brother Yu and Sister Chian who had once attended the Senior Fellowship and helped with the Youth Meeting and the baptisms. We enjoyed precious fellowship.

On Tuesday, September 8th, we went to the American Consulate. My daughter helped me fill out all the forms since I could not write with my right hand yet. I went to the window and handed in my papers, stating briefly my situation. I waited for some time while they studied my case. When the official came out and told me to return the next day for my visa, he asked me twice where I had learned my English. Obviously, he was surprised to hear an old Chinese woman speak such good English.

The next day we picked up the visa and purchased a ticket from the Northwest Airline office to fly to Seattle, and then Spokane, Washington on September 18. We did some shopping in the busy streets of Shanghai. On the way back to the train station, we chatted about how things had worked out so miraculously. We could see that God's hand had intervened. Though it had been an anxious wait and a zigzagging course, it turned out to be a wonderful credit to His glory. While the train cheerfully sped back to Nanjing and my daughter's knitting needles busily clicked, my thoughts turned this way and that as I anticipated the future. What would it feel like bidding farewell to my homeland and soaring above the clouds to a new place and people? The Lord had pointed out the way. I would follow in faith and spare no effort.

Epilogue

Julia Duan arrived in Spokane, Washington on September 19, 1992. After years of teaching, she returned to student life at Whitworth College and later at Moody Bible Institute. She studied Greek, the Gospel of John, Hermeneutics, English Writing and Christian World View, among many others. Her story was discovered by Linda Hunt, a writing professor at Whitworth, when she read Julia's description of her first night in the labor camp. Touched by this chapter in Julia's life, Linda suggested she write her entire story. The thought had never crossed Julia's mind and would have been impossible in China. She prayed and ultimately agreed to let her life "be a spectacle to the world for God's glory." Thus, Julia began a Herculean task which ushered her into the world of writing and computers. Spending eight to ten hours a day in the college computer lab, Julia learned how to use this new technology by trial and error. Since journals were not allowed in the labor camp, Julia set about writing her story from memory, first in English and then in Chinese. She squeezed writing time in between classes, studies, speaking engagements, and work.

During the last four years, Julia has been an ambassador for the believers of China. While at Whitworth, she gave her testimony in several community churches. She also participated in conferences for Chinese Christians in various cities. Her stories challenged and inspired these believers, most of whom converted to Christ after coming to the US.

In 1994, it came as a complete surprise to Julia when she was notified that the faculty of Whitworth College had voted to grant her a Bachelor of Arts degree in religion. On May 15, 1994, she donned cap and gown with the other graduates. Dr. Roger Mohrlang gave a speech of commendation and Julia walked across the stage to receive her diploma. The standing ovation by several thousand people showed the community's love and support for this woman whose life story has inspired so many.

Julia spent 1995 at Whitworth College working on her Chinese manuscript and serving on the chaplaincy team. In early 1996 she did graduate work at Moody Bible Institute and returned to China in November. Comparing her life to that of Abraham, Julia often says she is a pilgrim with the earth as her tent. Just as in China, she continues to "follow the Lord's leading and spare no effort." Now, at age 76 Julia's Chinese name, "to stand for the truth," still characterizes her life.